T0255121

Lecture Notes in Computer Science 13084

Founding Editors

Gerhard Goos
Karlsruhe Institute of Technology, Karlsruhe, Germany

Juris Hartmanis
Cornell University, Ithaca, NY, USA

Editorial Board Members

Elisa Bertino
Purdue University, West Lafayette, IN, USA

Wen Gao
Peking University, Beijing, China

Bernhard Steffen
TU Dortmund University, Dortmund, Germany

Gerhard Woeginger
RWTH Aachen, Aachen, Germany

Moti Yung
Columbia University, New York, NY, USA

More information about this subseries at https://link.springer.com/bookseries/7407

Gianlorenzo D'Angelo · Othon Michail (Eds.)

Algorithmic Aspects of Cloud Computing

6th International Symposium, ALGOCLOUD 2021
Lisbon, Portugal, September 6–7, 2021
Revised Selected Papers

Editors
Gianlorenzo D'Angelo
Gran Sasso Science Institute (GSSI)
L'Aquila, Italy

Othon Michail
University of Liverpool
Liverpool, UK

ISSN 0302-9743 ISSN 1611-3349 (electronic)
Lecture Notes in Computer Science
ISBN 978-3-030-93042-4 ISBN 978-3-030-93043-1 (eBook)
https://doi.org/10.1007/978-3-030-93043-1

LNCS Sublibrary: SL1 – Theoretical Computer Science and General Issues

© Springer Nature Switzerland AG 2021
This work is subject to copyright. All rights are reserved by the Publisher, whether the whole or part of the material is concerned, specifically the rights of translation, reprinting, reuse of illustrations, recitation, broadcasting, reproduction on microfilms or in any other physical way, and transmission or information storage and retrieval, electronic adaptation, computer software, or by similar or dissimilar methodology now known or hereafter developed.
The use of general descriptive names, registered names, trademarks, service marks, etc. in this publication does not imply, even in the absence of a specific statement, that such names are exempt from the relevant protective laws and regulations and therefore free for general use.
The publisher, the authors and the editors are safe to assume that the advice and information in this book are believed to be true and accurate at the date of publication. Neither the publisher nor the authors or the editors give a warranty, expressed or implied, with respect to the material contained herein or for any errors or omissions that may have been made. The publisher remains neutral with regard to jurisdictional claims in published maps and institutional affiliations.

This Springer imprint is published by the registered company Springer Nature Switzerland AG
The registered company address is: Gewerbestrasse 11, 6330 Cham, Switzerland

Preface

The International Symposium on Algorithmic Aspects of Cloud Computing (ALGOCLOUD) is an annual international symposium that aims to tackle the diverse new topics in the emerging area of algorithmic aspects of computing and data management in modern cloud-based systems, interpreted broadly so as to include edge- and fog-based systems, cloudlets, cloud micro-services, virtualization environments, and decentralized systems, as well as dynamic networks.

The symposium aims at bringing together researchers, students, and practitioners to present research activities and results on topics related to the algorithmic, design, and development aspects of modern cloud-based systems. ALGOCLOUD is particularly interested in novel algorithms in the context of cloud computing and cloud architectures, as well as experimental work that evaluates contemporary cloud approaches and pertinent applications. ALGOCLOUD also welcomes demonstration manuscripts, which discuss successful system developments, as well as experience/use-case articles and high-quality survey papers.

ALGOCLOUD 2021 took place during September 6–7, 2021 as a virtual event (due to the covid-19 pandemic), although it was originally planned to take place in Lisbon, Portugal. It was part of ALGO 2021 (September 6–10, 2021), the major annual congress that combines the premier algorithmic conference "European Symposium on Algorithms" (ESA) and a number of other specialized symposiums and workshops, all related to algorithms and their applications, making ALGO the major European event for researchers, students, and practitioners in algorithms.

There was a positive response to the ALGOCLOUD 2021 call for papers. The diverse nature of papers submitted demonstrated the vitality of the algorithmic aspects of cloud computing. All submissions went through a rigorous peer-review process and were reviewed by at least three Program Committee (PC) members. The submissions were evaluated based on their quality, originality, and relevance to the symposium. Following reviewers' recommendations, the PC accepted four original research papers and one brief announcement covering a variety of topics that were presented at the symposium. We would like to thank all PC members for their significant contribution to the review process.

The program of ALGOCLOUD 2021 was complemented with a keynote talk entitled "Cloud-Assisted Peer-to-Peer Systems", which was delivered by Christian Scheideler (Paderborn University, Germany), and three tutorials entitled "Self-Adjusting Networks: Enablers, Algorithms, Complexity", "Self-healing Distributed Algorithms", and "Gaming the Decentralized Finance", which were delivered by Stefan Schmid (University of Vienna, Austria), Amitabh Trehan (Durham University, UK), and Maria Potop-Butucaru (Sorbonne Université - LIP6), respectively. We wish to express our sincere gratitude to all our esteemed invitees for their contributions.

Finally, we would like to thank all authors who submitted their research work to ALGOCLOUD and the Steering Committee for its continuous support.

We hope that these proceedings will help researchers, students, and practitioners understand and be aware of state-of-the-art algorithmic aspects of cloud computing, and that they will stimulate further research in the domain of algorithmic approaches in cloud computing in general.

November 2021

Gianlorenzo D'Angelo
Othon Michail

Organization

Steering Committee

Spyros Sioutas	University of Patras, Greece
Peter Triantafillou	University of Warwick, UK
Christos D. Zaroliagis	University of Patras, Greece

Symposium Chairs

Gianlorenzo D'Angelo	Gran Sasso Science Institute, Italy
Othon Michail	University of Liverpool, UK

Program Committee

Janna Burman	Université Paris-Saclay, LISN, France
David Coudert	Inria, France
Giuseppe Di Luna	Sapienza University of Rome, Italy
Klaus-Tycho Foerster	University of Vienna, Austria
Chryssis Georgiou	University of Cyprus, Cyprus
Dariusz Kowalski	Augusta University, USA
Gianpiero Monaco	University of L'Aquila, Italy
Dennis Olivetti	University of Freiburg, Germany
Nikos Parotsidis	Google Zurich, Switzerland
Evaggelia Pitoura	University of Ioannina, Greece
Maria Potop-Butucaru	Sorbonne Université - LIP6, France
Amitabh Trehan	Durham University, UK
Kostas Tsichlas	University of Patras, Greece
Prudence Wong	University of Liverpool, UK

External Reviewer

Gagangeet Singh Aujla	Durham University, UK

Cloud-Assisted Peer-to-Peer Systems (Keynote Talk)

Christian Scheideler

Paderborn University, Germany
scheidel@mail.uni-paderborn.de

Abstract. Traditional approaches for distributed systems have either followed the client-server or peer-to-peer approach. However, with the emergence of clouds, another option becomes viable: cloud-assisted peer-to-peer systems. The idea behind cloud-assisted peer-to-peer systems is to combine the best of the client-server and the peer-to-peer approaches while avoiding their disadvantages by getting the cloud involved whenever the peer-to-peer system by itself cannot guarantee a desired quality of service. While cloud-assisted peer-to-peer systems have already been investigated by the systems community for more than a decade, in particular in the area of content streaming, these systems have not yet been studied in theory. In my presentation, I propose a model for cloud-assisted peer-to-peer systems and present various simple solutions for that model. A particularly interested aspect about this model is that whenever the cloud needs to get involved, the peers need to pay for that service, so the goal is to set up a solution so that the total amount of fees that needs to be paid for the cloud services is kept as small as possible while making sure that the fees from the peers cover the costs of the cloud.

Tutorials

Self-Adjusting Networks: Enablers, Algorithms, Complexity

Stefan Schmid

University of Vienna
stefan_schmid@univie.ac.at

Abstract. Network traffic is growing explosively, and next-generation workloads, e.g., related to (distributed) machine learning and artificial intelligence, will further increase the amount of traffic headed for and between the world's data centers. This quickly growing demand pushes today's wide-area and datacenter networks towards their capacity limits. While over the years, several interesting new network architectures have been proposed to improve the efficiency and performance of such networks, especially in the context of data centers, these networks often have in common that their topology is fixed and cannot be reconfigured to the traffic demand they serve. This tutorial discusses a different approach to operate networks: reconfigurable "self-adjusting" networks whose topology adjusts to the workload in an online manner. Reconfigurable networks are enabled by emerging optical technologies, allowing to quickly change the physical topology at runtime. This technology also introduces a vision of demand-aware networks which tap a new optimization opportunity: empirical and measurement studies show that traffic workloads feature spatial and temporal structure, which in principle could be exploited by reconfigurable networks. However, while the technology of such reconfigurable networks is evolving at a fast pace, these networks lack theoretical foundations: models, metrics, and algorithms - we have fallen behind the curve. The objective of this tutorial is to help bridge this gap, and introduce to the ALGO community a rich and potentially impactful research area, which touches many core topics of the conference. We first discuss technological enablers and report on motivating empirical studies. Our main focus in this tutorial then is on the new models and algorithmic challenges introduced by this field. In particular, we will review existing algorithms and complexity results, and highlight future research directions.

Self-healing Distributed Algorithms

Amitabh Trehan

Durham University, UK
amitabh.trehan@durham.ac.uk

Abstract. Resilience and fault-tolerance are highly desirable properties for networks and often distributed algorithms are designed with this purpose in mind. Self-healing is one such fault-tolerance paradigm which seeks to maintain a desirable state of the system despite attack accepting only a short disruption. The concept of self-healing appears in various forms ranging from autonomic networks to practical networks to distributed algorithms. We look at the later setting formalising self-healing as a game on graphs where a powerful adversary deletes/inserts nodes and the network responds by adding/dropping edges locally in a distributed manner while seeking to maintain global invariants. This requires the network to be reconfigurable e.g. in the P2P-CONGEST model (with limited message sizes). We look at various results in this setting building up self-healing resilience by adding topological properties such as connectivity, diameter, stretch, expansion, and routing in a simultaneous manner.

Gaming the Decentralized Finance

Maria Potop-Butucaru

Sorbonne Université - LIP6
maria.potop-butucaru@lip6.fr

Abstract. Decentralized finance opens a new research field: reliable distributed economical systems that is a cross research between classical distributed systems and mathematical models for economical systems. Blockchain technology is today at the core of decentralized finance. Differently from the classical distributed systems, blockchain technology faces complex faults and behaviors including rational. Interestingly, when rational behaviors are combined with classical faults (e.g. Byzantine behaviors) established results in distributed computing need to be revisited. This talk reports several results related to robustness of distributed abstractions used in blockchain technologies to Byzantine and rational behaviors analyzed through the lens of game theory.

Contents

On the Fault-Tolerant Online Bin Packing Problem 1
Shahin Kamali and Pooya Nikbakht

R-SWAP: Relay Based Atomic Cross-Chain Swap Protocol 18
Léonard Lys, Arthur Micoulet, and Maria Potop-Butucaru

New Results on Test-Cost Minimization in Database Migration 38
Utku Umur Acikalin, Bugra Caskurlu, Piotr Wojciechowski, and K. Subramani

Privately Querying Privacy: Privacy Estimation with Guaranteed Privacy of User and Database Party 56
Anna Katharina Hildebrandt, Ernst Althaus, and Andreas Hildebrandt

Brief Announcement: On the Distributed Construction of Stable Networks in Polylogarithmic Parallel Time 73
Matthew Connor

Author Index 81

On the Fault-Tolerant Online Bin Packing Problem

Shahin Kamali(✉) and Pooya Nikbakht(✉)

Department of Computer Science, University of Manitoba, Winnipeg, Canada
shahin.kamali@umanitoba.ca, nikbakhp@myumanitoba.ca

Abstract. We study the fault-tolerant variant of the online bin packing problem. Similar to the classic online bin packing problem, an online sequence of items of various sizes should be packed into a minimum number of bins of uniform capacity. For applications such as server consolidation, where bins represent servers and items represent jobs of various loads, it is necessary to maintain fault-tolerant solutions. In a fault-tolerant packing, any job is replicated into $f+1$ servers, for some integer $f > 1$, so that the failure of up to f servers does not interrupt service. We build over a practical model, introduced by Li and Tang [SPAA 2017], in which each job of load x has a primary replica of load x and f standby replicas, each of load x/η, where $\eta > 1$ is a parameter of the problem. Upon failure of up to f servers, any primary replica in a failed bin should be replaced by one of its standby replicas so that the extra load of the new primary replica does not cause an overflow in its bin.

We study a general setting in which bins might fail while the input is still being revealed. Our main contribution is an algorithm, named HARMONIC-STRETCH, which maintains fault-tolerant packings under this general setting. We prove that HARMONIC-STRETCH has an asymptotic competitive ratio of at most 1.75. This is an improvement over the best existing asymptotic competitive ratio 2 of an algorithm by Li and Tang [TPDS 2020], which works under a model that assumes bins fail only after all items are packed.

Keywords: Server consolidation · Online bin packing · Fault-tolerant bin packing · Competitive analysis

1 Introduction

Bin packing is a classic optimization problem with many applications and variants. In its basic form, the goal is to pack items of different sizes in the range $(0, 1]$ into the minimum number of bins of unit capacity. In doing so, an *offline* algorithm has access to all items before packing any of them, while an *online* algorithm receives items one by one and places each item into a bin without any prior knowledge about the forthcoming items. For example, FIRST-FIT is an online algorithm that places each item into the first bin that has enough space (and opens a new bin if no bin has enough space). The Harmonic family

© Springer Nature Switzerland AG 2021
G. D'Angelo and O. Michail (Eds.): ALGOCLOUD 2021, LNCS 13084, pp. 1–17, 2021.
https://doi.org/10.1007/978-3-030-93043-1_1

of algorithms, as another example of online algorithms, place items of similar sizes together in the same bins (see [7,12,14] for some variants of the Harmonic algorithm).

Server consolidation is an application of the online bin packing problem in the cloud. Service providers such as Amazon EC2 [6] or Microsoft Azure [2] host client applications, called *tenants*, on their servers. Upon the arrival of a tenant, an online algorithm assigns it to a server that has enough resources available for the tenant. For each tenant, the service provider commits to a Service Level Agreement (SLA) that specifies the minimum performance requirement for the tenant [15]. In particular, different tenants have various loads that are indicated in their SLAs. The goal of the service provider is to satisfy the SLA requirements while minimizing operational costs. To achieve this goal, cloud providers often *consolidate* tenants on shared computing machines to improve utilization [1]. Such consolidation can be modeled via online bin packing, where each item represents a tenant and each bin represents a computing machine (a server).

In cloud systems, client applications are often replicated in multiple servers. Such replication is necessary to avoid service interruptions in the case of server failures. In order to keep services uninterrupted against the failure of up to f services, it is necessary to replicate each tenant in at least $f+1$ different servers. In many practical scenarios, each tenant has a *primary* replica, which handles read/write queries, and multiple *standby* replicas, which act as backup replicas in anticipation of server failures. Naturally, the computational resources required for hosting primary replicas are more than that of standby replicas [16].

In this paper, we continue a line of research on the primary-standby scheme for the fault-tolerant bin packing problem [9,10]. The goal is to pack an online sequence of items (tenants) into a minimum number of bins (servers) such that each item of size x has a primary replica of size x and f standby replicas, each of size x/η, for some parameter $\eta > 1$. Over time, some servers might fail, and some of the previously failed servers might recover. An algorithm has no knowledge about how servers fail or recover, but it is guaranteed that the number of failed servers at each given time is at most f. To ensure the service is fault-tolerant, the primary replica of each job should be available at any given time. Therefore, when a server that hosts the primary replica of an item x fails, a standby replica of x should be selected to become its new primary replica. The subsequent increase in the load of such replica (from x/η to x) should not cause an overflow in the bin (see Sect. 2 for a formal definition).

The *asymptotic competitive ratio* is the standard measure for comparing online bin packing algorithms. An online algorithm A is said to have an asymptotic competitive ratio r iff for any sequence σ we have $A(\sigma) \leq r\ \textsc{Opt}(\sigma) + c$, where $A(\sigma)$ is the number of bins in the packing of A for σ, $\textsc{Opt}(\sigma)$ is the number of bins in an optimal *offline* packing of σ, and c is a constant independent of the length of σ. Throughout the paper, we use the term competitive ratio to refer to the asymptotic competitive ratio.

1.1 Previous Work and Contribution

Schaffner et al. [13] proposed the first model for the fault-tolerant bin packing problem and studied the competitiveness of a few basic algorithms. Subsequent work on this model resulted in improved algorithms [5,8,11]. These initial results studied a model in which the load of an item is evenly distributed between all its replicas. Li and Tang [9] introduced an alternative model that distinguishes between primary and standby replicas. This model was further studied in [10], where the HARMONIC-SHIFTING algorithm was presented and proved to have a competitive ratio of at most 2. All previous algorithms, in particular the HARMONIC-SHIFTING algorithm, assume that an online sequence is first packed and *then* a set of up to f bins might fail. In practice, however, the packing is an ongoing process, and the servers might fail while the input is still being revealed.

In this paper, we study the fault-tolerant bin packing problem with the primary-standby scheme, as introduced in [9]. We assume that bins can fail and recover in an online manner so that at most f bins are failed at the same time. As such, an algorithm in this model requires a *packing strategy*, which allocates items to bins, and an *adjustment strategy*, which makes necessary adjustments (i.e., promoting a standby replica to a primary replica and vice versa) when bins fail or recover. The packing and adjustment strategies should coordinate to maintain "valid" solutions that are tolerant against bin failures, that is, primary replicas are available for all items, and no bin is overloaded throughout the packing and adjustment processes.

We introduce an algorithm named HARMONIC-STRETCH that maintains fault-tolerant packings for an online sequence of items. As the prefix "Harmonic" suggests, HARMONIC-STRETCH classifies items by their sizes. The classification and treatment of items in each class is, however, different from the existing Harmonic-based algorithms. In particular, unlike the algorithms in [9,10], which classify items based on the size of their standby replicas, HARMONIC-STRETCH classifies items based on the size of their both primary and standby replicas. The placement and adjustment strategies in HARMONIC-STRETCH are designed in a flexible way that allows maintaining valid packings even if bins fail before the packing completes. We prove that HARMONIC-STRETCH has a competitive ratio of at most 1.75, which is an improvement over the competitive ratio 2 of HARMONIC-SHIFTING of [10]. In summary, HARMONIC-STRETCH is designed to work in a more general setting, and yet achieves a better competitive ratio when compared to the previous algorithms.

2 Primary-Standby Model for Fault-Tolerant Bin-Packing

The primary-standby scheme for the fault-tolerant bin packing problem is defined as follows:

Definition 1. *In the* (f, η)-fault-tolerant bin packing problem, *a sequence of* n *items, each having a size in the range* $(0, 1]$, *is revealed in an online manner. When an item of size* x *arrives, an algorithm places a* primary replica *of size* x

and f standby replicas, *each of size* x/η*, into bins of unit capacity, without any prior information about the forthcoming items. Throughout the packing process, some bins might fail and some of the previously failed bins might recover, in a way that the number of failed bins stays at most* f *at any time. In a valid packing, a primary replica of each item should be always available. Therefore, upon failure of a bin with a primary replica of an item* x*, a standby replica of* x *(in a non-failed bin) needs to be selected and promoted to become the new primary replica of* x*. The subsequent increase in the size of the promoted standby replica (from* x/η *to* x*) should not cause an overload in any bin. The objective is to maintain a valid packing with a minimum number of bins.*

We assume that the packing of the $f+1$ replicas of any item takes place concurrently, that is, no bin fails when a group of $f+1$ replicas is being packed. Note that an algorithm can change the status of a replica from primary to standby and vice versa, but it cannot move replicas from one bin to another. In order to achieve a valid packing, the $f+1$ replicas of each item need to be packed in $f+1$ different bins; otherwise, failure of up to f bins that contain all replicas of an item makes that item inaccessible.

Example 1. Figure 1 illustrates Definition 1. Each item of size x has a primary replica of size x and $f = 2$ standby replicas of size x/η, where $\eta = 2.0$. The packing (a) is a valid packing. The failure of any single bin or a pair of bins at any time can be addressed by promoting a standby replica into a primary replica without overloading any bin. For example, the arrows in the figure point to the standby replicas that are selected to become primary replicas after the simultaneous failure of bins B_1 and B_2 at time t_1. The packing (b), on the other hand, is not a valid packing of σ: if B_1 and B_2 fail, it is not possible to select standby replicas to replace the failed primary replicas without overloading a bin.

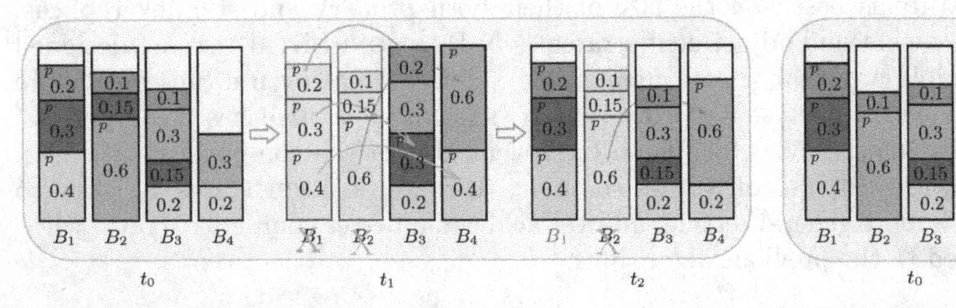

(a) A valid solution: four items are packed at time t_0. Bins B_1 and B_2 fail at time t_1, and standby replicas in other bins replace primary replicas in the failed bins. B_1 recovers at t_2, and the algorithm gives back the primary status to replicas in B_1.

(b) An invalid solution at time t_0.

Fig. 1. Packing sequence $\sigma = (0.4, 0.6, 0.3, 0.2)$, where $f = 2$ and $\eta = 2.0$. Replicas of the same items have the same color; primary replicas have the letter p.

3 Harmonic-Stretch Algorithm

In this section, we present the Harmonic-Stretch algorithm. First, we provide an overview of the main components of the algorithm.

Item Classification: Items are partitioned into *classes*, based on the size of their primary and standby replicas. There are 7 possible classes for primary replicas and $\lfloor 6\eta \rfloor + 1$ classes for standby replicas. An item that has a primary replica of class i ($1 \leq i \leq 7$) and a standby replica of class j ($1 \leq j \leq \lfloor 6\eta \rfloor + 1$) is called an (i, j)-items. When $i = 7$ and $j = \lfloor 6\eta \rfloor + 1$, the (i, j)-items are called *small items*, while other items are called *regular items* (see Sect. 3.1 for details).

Items that have the same primary and standby classes are packed separately from other items, that is, a replica of an (i, j)-item is never placed with a replica of an (i', j')-item together in the same bin if $i \neq i'$ or $j \neq j'$.

Maintaining Bin Groups: To place (i, j)-items, the algorithm maintains *groups* of bins. Each group is formed by a constant number of (initially empty) bins. At any given time, there is one "active" group for (i, j)-items, where the incoming (i, j)-items are packed into. When no more items can fit into the active group, the group becomes "complete", and another group becomes the active group. If a bin of the active group fails, the algorithm declares that group as "unavailable", leaves that group "incomplete" and selects a new active group. When all failed bins of an incomplete group recover, that group becomes "available" again. When a new active group is required (i.e., when the currently active group becomes complete or one of its bins fails), an (incomplete) available group is selected as the new active group. If no available group exists, the algorithm opens a fresh group with empty bins as the active group. Given that at most f bins can fail at the same time, the algorithm maintains up to $f + 1$ incomplete groups for (i, j)-items, out of which one group is the active group, and f groups are either unavailable or include bins that have recovered from a failure (see Sect. 3.2).

Packing Strategy: When placing (i, j)-items inside their active group, primary and standby replicas are packed in separate bins, which are respectively called *primary* and *standby bins*. Items in primary bins are packed as tightly as possible, while items in the standby bins are packed so that there is enough space for the promotion of exactly one replica. The packing strategy ensures that a primary bin shares replicas of at most one item with any standby bin. For small items, a consecutive number of them are merged to form "super-replicas"; each super-replica is treated in the same way that regular items are packed (see Sect. 3.3).

Adjustment Strategy: When a bin B fails, for each primary replica x in B, a standby replica of x in a non-failed bin should be promoted to become the new primary replica. This is done through maintaining an injective mapping h. The domain of h is the set of primary replicas like x residing in the primary bins that are failed, and the range of h is a set of non-failed standby bins in the same group such that $h(x)$ contains a standby replica of x. The injective nature

Table 1. A summary of the replica classes used in the definition and analysis of the HARMONIC-STRETCH algorithm. The weight and density of classes is used in the analysis of the algorithm.

primary replicas				standby replicas			
class	size	weight	density	class	size	weight	density
$i = 1$	$(\frac{1}{2}, 1]$	1	< 2	$j = 1$	$(\frac{1}{\eta+1}, \frac{1}{\eta}]$	1	$< \eta + 1$
$i = 2$	$(\frac{1}{3}, \frac{1}{2}]$	$\frac{1}{2}$	$< \frac{3}{2}$	$j = 2$	$(\frac{1}{\eta+2}, \frac{1}{\eta+1}]$	$\frac{1}{2}$	$< \frac{\eta+2}{2}$
$\vdots$	$\vdots$	$\vdots$	$\vdots$	$\vdots$	$\vdots$	$\vdots$	$\vdots$
$i \in [1, 5]$	$(\frac{1}{i+1}, \frac{1}{i}]$	$\frac{1}{i}$	$< \frac{i+1}{i}$	$j \in [1, \lfloor 6\eta \rfloor - 1]$	$(\frac{1}{\eta+j}, \frac{1}{\eta+j-1}]$	$\frac{1}{j}$	$< \frac{\eta+j}{j}$
$i = 6$	$(\frac{1}{7-1/\eta}, \frac{1}{6}]$	$\frac{1}{6}$	$< \frac{7}{6}$	$j = \lfloor 6\eta \rfloor$	$(\frac{1}{7\eta-1}, \frac{1}{\eta+\lfloor 6\eta \rfloor-1}]$	$\frac{1}{\lfloor 6\eta \rfloor}$	$< \frac{\eta+\lfloor 6\eta \rfloor}{\lfloor 6\eta \rfloor}$
$i = 7$	$p \in (0, \frac{1}{7-1/\eta}]$	$\frac{3}{2}p$	$\frac{3}{2}$	$j = \lfloor 6\eta \rfloor + 1$	$s \in (0, \frac{1}{7\eta-1}]$	$\frac{3}{2}s$	$\frac{3}{2}$

of the mapping, and the fact that there is enough space for expansion of one standby replica in $h(x)$, implies that one can promote the standby replica in $h(x)$ to replace x as the primary replica, without causing an overflow in $h(x)$. The assignment of standby replicas as primary replicas is temporary, that is, upon the recovery of B, its primary replicas like x will retain their primary status and are removed from the domain of h, while the promoted replica in $h(x)$ is demoted to become a standby replicas again (see Sect. 3.4).

In what follows, we explain the above components in more detail.

3.1 Item Classification

There are seven classes for primary replicas and $\lfloor 6\eta \rfloor + 1$ classes for standby replicas (see Table 1 for details). An item has *primary class* $i \in \{1, 2, 3, 4, 5\}$ if its primary replica is of size in the range $(\frac{1}{i+1}, \frac{1}{i}]$, primary class 6 if its primary replica is of size in the range $(\frac{1}{7-1/\eta}, \frac{1}{6}]$, and primary class 7 if its primary replica is of size at most $\frac{1}{7-1/\eta}$. We refer to items of primary class $i \leq 6$ as *regular* items, and items of primary class 7 as *small* items. An item has *standby class* $j \in \{1, 2, \ldots, \lfloor 6\eta \rfloor - 1\}$ if its standby replica has size in the range $(\frac{1}{j+\eta}, \frac{1}{j+\eta-1}]$, standby class $j = \lfloor 6\eta \rfloor$ if its standby class has size in the range $(\frac{1}{7\eta-1}, \frac{1}{\lfloor 6\eta \rfloor+\eta-1}]$, and standby class $\lfloor 6\eta \rfloor + 1$ if its standby replica is of size $\frac{1}{7\eta-1}$.

In what follows, we refer to an item of primary class i and standby class j as an (i, j)-items. Primary replicas of small items (with $i = 7$) are in the range $(0, \frac{1}{7-1/\eta}]$, and their standby replicas are in the range $(0, \frac{1}{7\eta-1}]$. Therefore, an (i, j)-item is a small item if $i = 7$ and $j = \lfloor 6\eta \rfloor + 1$, and a regular item otherwise.

3.2 Maintaining Bin Groups

For each pair of i, j, the algorithm maintains one group of bins, which are all non-failed, as the *active* group. As (i, j)-items are revealed, they are packed into bins of the active group, as will be explained in Sect. 3.3. In the beginning, a group of all-empty bins is opened and declared as the active group for (i, j)-items. A new active group is needed when either i) one of the bins in the active group fails or ii) enough items are placed inside the active group, and the group becomes *complete*; before that, the group is *incomplete*. A group is said to be *available* if none of its bins are failed. An active group is always available. When a new active group is required, the algorithm checks whether an incomplete and available group exists. Such a group, if it exists, is a former active group that, at some point lost its active status due to a bin failure. Since the group is now available, its failed bins are now recovered. If such a group exists, it is selected as the new active group (if multiple such groups exist, one is chosen arbitrarily). On the other hand, if no incomplete, available group exists, the algorithm opens a fresh group of all-empty bins and declares it as the active group.

Lemma 1. *There are at most $f+1$ incomplete groups at each given time during the execution of the algorithm.*

Proof. Consider otherwise, that is, at some point, there are at least $f+2$ incomplete groups. Let t denote the time at which the $(f+2)$'th group G is initiated. There are at most f groups that contain at least one failed bin at any given time, in particular, at time t. So, out of the $f+1$ incomplete groups at time t (before G is initiated), at least one group G' has been incomplete and available. Therefore, G' had to be selected as the new active group instead of G, a contradiction. □

3.3 Packing Strategy

We explain how the algorithm packs (i, j)-items inside their active group. The placement is slightly different for regular and small items:

Regular Items. We describe how (i, j)-items are packed, where $i \leq 6$ and $j \leq \lfloor 6\eta \rfloor$. Each bin group for (i, j)-items, in particular the active group, is formed by $j + fi$ bins and has enough space for ij items. The group becomes complete when ij items are placed in it. There are j primary bins $B_0, B_1, \ldots, B_{j-1}$ that are each partitioned into i *spots* of capacity $1/i$. There are fi standby bins formed by f sets of bins, each containing i standby bins. We use $\beta_0^k, \beta_1^k, \ldots \beta_{i-1}^k$ to denote the standby bins in the k'th set ($k \leq f$). Each standby bin is partitioned into j spots of size $\frac{1}{j+\eta-1}$. This leaves a *reserved space* of size $\frac{\eta-1}{j+\eta-1}$ in the bin. The spots in the standby bins are labeled from 0 to $j-1$.

Let a_t be the t'th item that is to be packed into the group ($0 \leq t \leq ij-1$). Let $w = (t \mod j)$ and $z = \lfloor t/j \rfloor$. Note that w and z are in the ranges $[0, j-1]$ and $[0, i-1]$, respectively. The algorithm places the primary replica of a_t in the spot z of the primary bin B_w in the active group. Standby replicas of a_t are placed in the spot w of bins $\beta_z^1, \beta_z^2, \ldots, \beta_z^f$ of the active group.

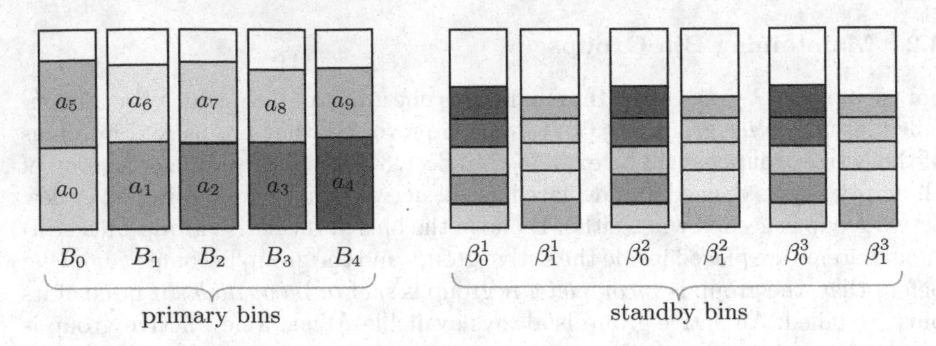

Fig. 2. An illustration of the HARMONIC-STRETCH packing for regular (i, j)-items in a complete group, where $i = 2$, $j = 5$, and $f = 3$.

Example 2. Figure 2 illustrates packing items of class (i, j), where $i = 2$, $j = 5$, and $f = 3$ in a complete group. There are $j = 5$ primary bins $B_0, \ldots, B_4$, each partitioned into $i = 2$ spots. There are $f = 3$ groups of standby bins, each containing $i = 2$ bins that are partitioned into $j = 5$ spots. For an item like a_4 (the red item), we have $w = 4$ and $z = 0$. The primary replica of a_4 is thus placed in the 0'th spot of the 4'th bin, while standby replicas of a_4 are placed in the 4'th spot of the bin β_0^k for $k \in [1, 3]$.

Example 3. Figure 3 shows an incomplete group of bins opened for (i, j)-items where $i = 2$, $j = 5$, and $f = 3$. The group includes $j + fi = 11$ bins. Each of the primary bins and standby bins has $i = 2$ and $j = 6$ spots, respectively, out of which the black spots have not been filled yet. The algorithm has placed items $a_0, \ldots a_6$ in their respective bins when the group was active (and , hence, available). At some time t, bins B_0 and B_4 failed. At this point, the group becomes unavailable, and the adjustment strategy processes a_0, a_5, and a_4 to assign new primary replicas for them. After time t, the group will not be active anymore (because it is not available), and the algorithm does not place upcoming items in this group until it is selected as the active group later again; this requires the group to become available again, that is, B_0 and B_4 recover.

Small Items. In order to pack replicas of small items, HARMONIC-STRETCH merges sets of consecutive small items into *super-replicas* (SRs). Given that the size of small primary and standby replicas are respectively at most $\frac{1}{7-1/\eta}$ and $\frac{1}{7\eta-1}$, it is possible to group consecutive primary and standby replicas into SRs with sizes in the range $(\frac{1}{7-1/\eta}, \frac{2}{7-1/\eta})$ and $(\frac{1}{7\eta-1}, \frac{2}{7\eta-1})$, respectively. The algorithm maintains an (initially empty) *open* primary SR of capacity $\frac{2}{7-1/\eta}$ and places consecutive primary replicas in the open SR until placing the next replica causes the total size of replicas in the SR to exceed its capacity. At this point, the SR is closed and a new SR is opened. Similarly, the algorithm maintains f (initially empty) open standby SRs, each of capacity $\frac{2}{7\eta-1}$, and places the f

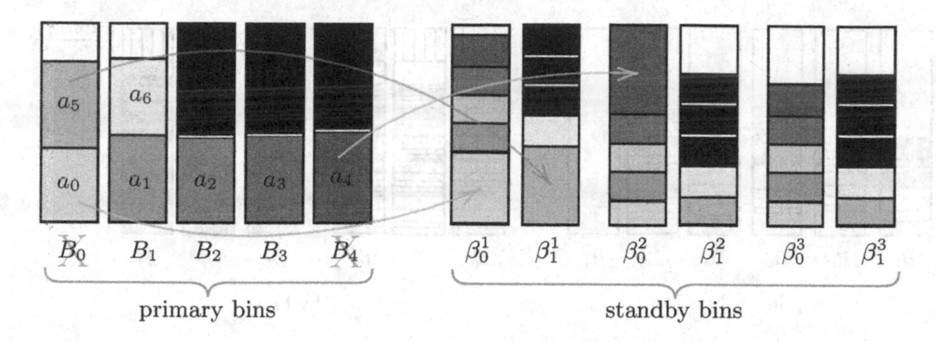

Fig. 3. An unavailable and incomplete group of bins for (i, j)-items, where $i = 2$, $j = 5$, and $f = 3$.

standby replicas in these bins until a replica does not fit the open SRs, at which point the f open SRs are closed and a set of f new SRs are opened. Since the primary and standby SRs are opened and closed at the same time, we can think of a set of small replicas that are placed in an SR as a single regular replica. In what follows, we describe how the newly opened SRs are placed into bins.

Each group G of bins opened for small items contains f standby bins that mirror each other[1] and one primary replica which is "committed" to G. There are also "free" primary bins that are not committed to any group. Upon the arrival of a small item, its standby replicas are placed into the open SRs located on (mirroring bins) of the active group, and its primary replica is placed into the open SR located on the committed bin. As before, if any bin of the active group fails, the group becomes unavailable, and the algorithm declares another incomplete, available group as the active group (or creates a new one if no such group exists). There is a reserved space of size $\frac{2(\eta-1)}{7\eta-1} + \frac{2}{7\eta-1} = \frac{2(\eta-1)}{7\eta-1}$ inside each of the f mirroring bins of a group, which is used for the promotion of the standby SRs when required. When it is needed to open a new SR (when the new replicas do not fit in the open SR), HARMONIC-STRETCH first places f standby SRs and then a single primary SR as follows. For the f standby SRs, if the available space in the mirroring standby bins of the active group is at least $\frac{2\eta}{7\eta-1}$, then the new SRs will be placed into the existing open standby bins. Otherwise, the active group gets complete, and either another incomplete, available group is selected as the active group, or (if there is no such an available group) a new group is opened. For placing a new primary SR, the algorithm first frees the bin committed to the active group, and then selects any free primary bin B' that i) has an empty space of size at least $\frac{2}{7-1/\eta}$ and ii) is not sharing an SR with any of the f standby bins in the active group. If no such bin B' exists, the algorithm opens a new primary bin B'. The bin B' is then declared as the new primary bin committed to the active group, where the new primary SR is placed.

[1] Two bins "mirror" each other iff they contain the same set of replicas.

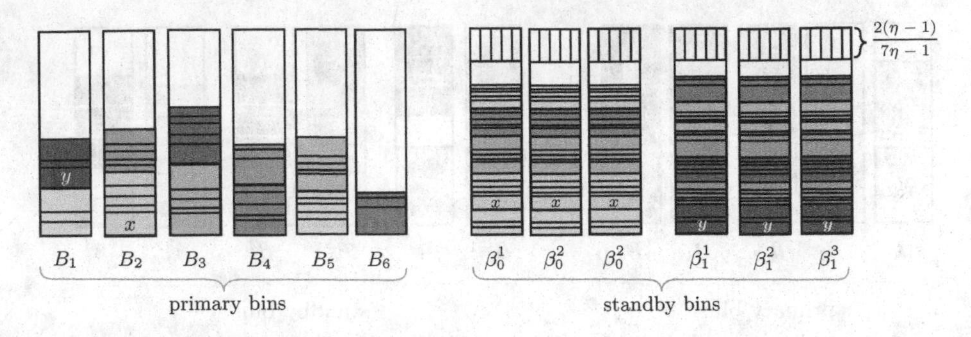

Fig. 4. An illustration of the HARMONIC-STRETCH packing for placing small items, where $f = 3$.

Example 4. Figure 4 illustrates how HARMONIC-STRETCH packs small items, where $\eta = 2$ and $f = 3$. Replicas of items that form the same SR have the same color. SRs of primary replicas have sizes in the range $(\frac{1}{7-1/\eta}, \frac{2}{7-1/\eta})$, that is, $(2/13, 4/13)$. Standby SRs have sizes in the range $(\frac{1}{7\eta-1}, \frac{2}{7\eta-1})$, that is, $(1/13, 2/13)$. The algorithm maintains a reserved space of $\frac{2(\eta-1)}{7\eta-1} = 2/13$ inside each standby bin. The initial small items are placed into the yellow SRs. Note that the standby SRs are placed in $f = 3$ open mirroring bins (β_0^1, β_0^2, and β_0^3) and the primary SR is placed in bin B_1, which is the initially committed bin to the active group. At some point, replicas of an item x do not fit in the standby SRs of the active group (the total size of primary and standby yellow replicas exceeds $\frac{4}{13}$ and $\frac{2}{13}$, respectively, if replicas of x are included in the yellow SRs.). As such, a new SR (the light green SR) is opened for x. Given that the empty and non-reserved space in the mirroring bins of the current group is enough to fit another standby SR of size at most $2/13$, the standby replicas of the new SR are placed in the open mirroring bins. Meanwhile, B_1 is freed, and a new bin B_2 is selected as the new committed primary bin to the active group, where the new primary SR is placed. Note that B_1 is freed because it already shares yellow SR with the standby bins of the active group. Similarly, the standby replicas of the subsequent SRs (of colors orange, blue, and pink) are placed in the mirroring bins of the active group while their primary replicas are placed in separate primary bins (each becoming the new committed bins upon freeing the previous one). At some point, replicas of some item y cannot fit in the current (pink) SRs. So, a new SR (of color red) needs to be opened. The current mirroring bins do not have an available space of $\frac{2}{7\eta-1} = 2/13$; as such, the active group gets complete, and a new group with $f = 3$ standby bins (β_1^1, β_1^2, and β_1^3) is opened, where the new standby SRs are placed. At this point, the primary replica of the new SR (the red SR) can be placed in any of the primary bins B_1 to B_6, that is, any of B_1 to B_6 can be selected as the committed bin to the new active group. This is because none of these primary bins are related to this new set of open standby bins. In the figure, B_1 is initially selected as the primary bin committed to the new group.

3.4 Adjustment Strategy

We describe an adjustment strategy that ensures a primary replica is available at any given time during the execution of HARMONIC-STRETCH.

Two bins in the packing of HARMONIC-STRETCH are said to be *related through item* x if they both contain (primary or standby) replicas of item x. Clearly, any two related bins should belong to the same group of bins.

Lemma 2. *In a packing maintained by* HARMONIC-STRETCH, *if a primary bin* B_p *is related to a standby bin* β_1 *through an item* x *and to a standby bin* β_2 *through an item* $y \neq x$, *then* β_1 *and* β_2 *are not related through any item.*

Proof. Let $\mathcal{P}$ be the packing maintained by HARMONIC-STRETCH. First, we show that (i) any pair of standby bins that are related mirror each other, and (ii) any primary bin in $\mathcal{P}$ shares replicas of at most one item with any standby bin. For (i), note that the algorithm places the standby replicas of each regular item in bins that mirror each other. The same holds for the small replicas because the standby SRs are placed into mirroring bins (see Figs. 2 and 4). For small items, (ii) follows directly from the definition of the HARMONIC-STRETCH. This is because the algorithm places each primary SR into a primary bin that does not share an SR with any (standby) bin of the active group. We use proof by contradiction to prove (ii) for the regular items. Assume a primary bin B includes primary replicas of items x and y of class (i, j) while a standby bin β' also includes replicas of x and y. Given that x and y are regular items, they belong to the same set of the ij items that are placed in the same group (with $j + fi$ bins) in $\mathcal{P}$. Let t_x and t_y respectively denote the indices of x and y in the group ($t_x \neq t_y$). Since x and y have their primary replicas in B, we should have ($t_x \mod j$)$=$ ($t_y \mod j$). Similarly, since their standby replicas are placed in β', we should have $\lfloor t_x/j \rfloor = \lfloor t_y/j \rfloor$. This contradicts $t_x \neq t_y$.

Provided with (i) and (ii), we are ready to prove the lemma. Suppose the lemma does not hold, that is, a primary bin B_p in $\mathcal{P}$ is related to a standby bin β_1 through an item x and to standby bin β_2 through an item y ($y \neq x$), while β_1 and β_2 are also related. Since β_1 and β_2 are related, by (i), they should mirror each other, that is, β_1 includes replicas of both x and y, and so does β_2. Thus, B_p shares replicas of both x and y with β_1 (and β_2), contradicting (ii). □

We use Lemma 2 to develop the adjustment strategy of HARMONIC-STRETCH:

Theorem 1. *There is an adjustment strategy that ensures the packing of* HARMONIC-STRETCH *stays valid, that is, a primary replica of each item is always present in a non-failed bin.*

Proof. We describe an adjustment strategy that maintains an injective mapping h that maps each primary replica x placed originally in a failed primary bin into a non-failed standby bin $h(x)$ which hosts a standby replica of the same item. For each primary replica x in a failed primary bin, the standby replica in $h(x)$ replaces x as the new primary replica. Since the mapping is injective, at most one replica in each standby bin will be promoted to a primary replica. Given that each standby bin with a replica of size s has an empty space of at least $(\eta - 1)s$, no bin is overloaded. In what follows, we describe an adjustment strategy that maintains the desired injective mapping as bins fail and recover. In this process, the standby bins that are in the range of h are referred to as "marked" bins.

We describe how to maintain the mapping h at time t. Suppose that such mapping is maintained in the previous $t-1$ steps. Let f_p denote the number of primary bins that are failed (and not recovered) before time t (we have $0 \leq f_p \leq f$). Suppose that out of these f_p failed primary bins, r_p bins are recovered at time t ($0 \leq r_p \leq f_p$). A bin B is said to be *critical* iff it fails at time t while containing a primary replica. Let k denote the number of critical bins. All primary bins that fail at time t are critical (non-failed primary bins contain primary replicas). Marked standby bins that fail at time t are also critical (they are in the range of h and hence a replica in them has replaced the primary replica of a failed primary bin). For the packing to stay valid, the primary replicas in the critical bins should be mapped to some non-failed bins.

The adjustment algorithm first ensures that the primary replicas in the r_p recovered primary bins are removed from the domain of h, and retain their primary status; this means the standby replicas in the range of h that were previously upgraded to primary replicas become standby again and their bins become unmarked. At this point, the number of failed, unmarked standby bins is at most $f - (f_p - r_p + k)$; this is because, out of at most f failed bins, $f_p - r_p$ of them are primary bins that are failed before t, and k of them are critical and hence are either primary bins or marked standby bins.

Consider an arbitrary ordering $(B_1, B_2, \ldots, B_k)$ of the critical bins. We process the critical bins, one by one, in this order. When processing a bin B_q, we process primary replicas in B_q in an arbitrary order ($q \leq k$). Let a be a replica in B_q that is being processed, and let A be the set of f standby bins that include replicas of a. We need to map a to an unmarked bin $\beta \in A$ and then mark β. We show that it is always possible to find such an unmarked bin β. Consider a previously processed bin B' (whose primary replicas are mapped), that is, either B' failed previously at $t' < t$ or B' is $B_{q'}$ for $q' < q$. We claim that during the process of B', at most one bin from A has become marked. At the time B' is processed, it has been critical and hence either a primary bin or a marked standby bin. If B' was a marked standby bin, then it contained at most one primary replica (since the mapping is injective), and the claim holds. To prove the claim when B' is a primary bin, consider otherwise, that is, assume two standby bins $\beta_x, \beta_y \in A$ have been marked during the process of B' . This means B' is related to β_x and β_y through two different items. On the other hand, β_x and β_y are also related to each other (because they are both in A and hence contain a replica of a). This is not possible, however, given the result in Lemma 2.

There are $f_p - r_p + q - 1$ failed bins that are processed before B_q. By the above argument, processing any of these bins results in marking at most one standby bin from A. Therefore, at the time of processing a, at most $f_p - r_p + q - 1$ standby bins from A are previously marked. Note that a is replicated on f standby bins. As a result, there are at least $f - f_p + r_p - q + 1$ unmarked standby bins that host standby replicas of a. Among these bins, at most $f-(f_p+r_p-k)$ bins are failed. So, there are at least $f-f_p+r_p-q+1-(f-f_b+r_p-k)=k-q+1$ non-failed and unmarked standby bins in A. Given that $q \leq k$, there is at least one unmarked bin that a can be mapped to. □

4 Competitiveness of HARMONIC-STRETCH

In this section, we use a weighting argument to provide an upper bound for the competitive ratio of HARMONIC-STRETCH. We assign a *weight* to each replica in the final packing of the algorithm. The weights are defined in a way that the total weight of replicas placed in each bin of the algorithm, except possibly a constant number of them, is at least 1. Therefore, if $w(\sigma)$ denotes the total weight of all replicas in the input sequence, the number of bins in the packing of HARMONIC-STRETCH is no more than $w(\sigma)+c$, for some constant c independent of the input length (but possibly a function of parameters f and η). At the same time, we show that any bin in an optimal packing has a weight at most 1.75, which means the number of bins in an optimal packing is at least $w(\sigma)/1.75$. As such, the competitive ratio of HARMONIC-STRETCH will be at most 1.75.

Weighting: For regular items, define the weight of a primary replica of class i (≤ 6) as $1/i$, and the weight of standby replicas of class j ($\leq \lfloor 6\eta \rfloor$) as $1/j$. For small items, a primary or standby replica of size x has weight $3x/2$ (see Table 1).

Lemma 3. *The total weight of replicas in any bin of* HARMONIC-STRETCH, *except for at most a constant number of bins, is at least 1.*

Proof. First, we investigate regular bins. Consider the bins in the complete groups (see Fig. 2). In any such group, a primary bin of class $i \leq 6$ includes i replicas, each of weight $1/i$. Similarly, a standby bin of class $j \leq \lfloor 6\eta \rfloor$ includes j replicas, each of weight $1/j$. Therefore, all regular bins, except for those in the incomplete groups, have weight 1. We show that the total number of bins inside incomplete groups is a constant independent of the input length. By Lemma 1, there are at most $f+1$ incomplete groups for (i,j)-items. There are $j+fi \leq 6(\eta+f)$ bins inside each group. So, there are at most $6(f+1)(\eta+f)$ partially-filled bins for (i,j)-items. Given that $i \leq 6$ and $j \leq 6\eta$, there are at most 36η possible pairs of (i,j). In total, the number of partially filled bins for regular items is at most $(36\eta)6(f+1)(\eta+f)=O(1)$. In summary, the total weight of items in any regular bin, except for at most $O(1)$ of them, is at least 1.

Next, we look into small items. Let x be the primary SR that causes opening the last primary small bin. Also, let m be the number of standby SRs packed in the standby bins of the active group at the time x was placed. There are m primary bins that are related to the f standby bins, and thus cannot host x. By Lemma 1, there are up to f incomplete groups other than the active group. The primary bins committed to these groups also cannot host x. The remaining primary bins could not host x only because they did not have enough space.

So, all primary small bins, except at most $m+f$ of them, are filled to a level of at least $1-\frac{2}{7-1/\eta}=\frac{5\eta-1}{7\eta-1}\geq 2/3$. Given that any small item of size s has weight $1.5s$, the total weight of replicas in any of these bins is at least $1.5\ (2/3)=1$. Next, we show that m is a constant with respect to the input length. Each standby bin has a non-reserved space of size $1-\frac{2(\eta-1)}{7\eta-1}=\frac{5\eta+1}{7\eta-1}$ which is used to pack SRs of size at least $\frac{1}{7\eta-1}$. As such, we have $m\leq 5\eta+1$. So, all primary small bins, except for at most $5\eta+1+f\in O(1)$ of them, have weight at least 1. Standby small bins have a reserved space of $\frac{2(\eta-1)}{7\eta-1}$. Except for the bins inside the incomplete groups, other bins have an additional empty space of at most $\frac{2}{7\eta-1}$, giving them a total empty space of at most $\frac{2\eta}{7\eta-1}$. By Lemma 1, there are up to $f+1$ incomplete groups, each containing f mirroring bins. Therefore, the filled space in each standby bin, except for at most $f(f+1)=O(1)$ of them, is at least $\frac{5\eta-1}{7\eta-1}\geq 2/3$. Given that any standby small replica of size s has weight $1.5s$, the weight of any of these standby bins is then at least $1.5\ (3/2)=1$. □

Lemma 4. *The total weight of items in any bin of an optimal packing is at most 1.75.*

Proof. Define the *density* of each item as the ratio between the weight and the size of the item. A primary replica of class $i\leq 6$ has a size in the range $(\frac{1}{i+1},\frac{1}{i}]$ and weight $1/i$, which gives a density of at most $\frac{i+1}{i}$. Similarly, standby replicas of class $j\leq\lfloor 6\eta\rfloor$ have size in the range $(\frac{1}{j+\eta},\frac{1}{j+\eta-1}]$ and weight $1/j$, giving them a density of at most $(j+\eta)/j$. Small replicas (both primary and standby) have a density of $3/2$. We consider three possible cases and show that the total weight of items in any bin B^* of an optimal packing is at most 1.75 in each case. To follow the proof, it helps to consult Table 1.

Case 1: No Standby Replica in B^*: Suppose B^* does not include any standby replica. In this case, B^* includes 0 or 1 primary replica of class 1 (it cannot include more than 1 such replica since all replicas of class 1 have sizes larger than $1/2$). If it includes no replica of class 1, the density of each of the items (of other classes) is at most 1.5, giving a total weight of at most 1.5 for items in B^*. If B^* includes one item of class 1 (with weight 1), the total size of other items will be less than $1/2$, and since their density is at most $3/2$, their total weight will be no more than $3/2\cdot 1/2=3/4$, giving a total weight of at most $1+3/4=1.75$ for items in B^*.

Case 2: Some Standby Replicas in B^* Are Regular: Suppose B^* includes at least one regular standby replica. Let x be the largest standby replica in B^* and j denote the class of x; we have $1\leq j\leq\lfloor 6\eta\rfloor$. There should be enough empty space in B^* so that if all f bins containing other replicas of x are failed, x can be declared as a primary replica. Increasing the size of x by a factor η should not cause an overflow, that is, there should be empty space of at least $(\eta-1)x>(\eta-1)/(j+\eta)$ in B^* (recall that replicas of class j are of sizes at least $1/(j+\eta)$). So, the total size of items in B^* is less than $1-\frac{\eta-1}{j+\eta}=\frac{j+1}{j+\eta}$. There are two cases to consider: either $j=1$ or $j\geq 2$:

i) Suppose $j = 1$, that is, there is a standby replica x of size more than $1/(1+\eta)$ in B^*. The total size of items in the bin is less than $\frac{j+1}{j+\eta} = \frac{2}{\eta+1}$, and items other than x in B^* have a total size less than $\frac{1}{\eta+1}$. As a result, there is no primary replica of class 1 (of size at least $1/2 > \frac{1}{\eta+1}$) or standby replica of class 1 (of size more than $\frac{1}{\eta+1}$) in B^*. So, primary replicas in B^* have class 2 or more and hence density at most 1.5. Similarly, standby replicas other than x have class 2 or more and hence density no more than $\frac{\eta+2}{2}$. So, all replicas other than x in B^* have a density at most $\max\{1.5, \frac{\eta+2}{2}\} = \frac{\eta+2}{2}$. Since the total size of these replicas is at most $\frac{1}{\eta+1}$, their total weight is at most $\frac{1}{\eta+1} \cdot \frac{\eta+2}{2} = \frac{\eta+2}{2\eta+2}$. Adding the weight 1 of x, the total weight of replicas in B^* is at most $\frac{3\eta+4}{2\eta+2}$, which is at most 1.75, given that $\eta > 1$.

ii) Suppose $j \geq 2$. Recall that the total size of items in B^* is less than $\frac{j+1}{j+\eta}$. First, assume there is also a primary replica y of class 1 in B^*. This is possible only if $\frac{1}{j+\eta} + \frac{1}{2} < \frac{j+1}{j+\eta}$, that is, $\eta < j$. The size of replicas other than y in B^* is less than $\frac{j+1}{j+\eta} - 1/2 = \frac{j+2-\eta}{2j+2\eta}$, and their density is at most $\max\{1.5, (j+\eta)/j\}$ (primary replicas of class ≥ 2 have density at most 3/2, and standby replicas have density at most $(j+\eta)/j$). The total weight of replicas other than y is hence less than $\max\{\frac{3j+6-3\eta}{4j+4\eta}, \frac{j+2-\eta}{2j}\} \leq \max\{3/4, \frac{j+2-\eta}{2j}\}$, which is at most 0.75, given that $\eta > 1$ and $j \geq 2$. Adding the weight 1 of y, the total weight of replicas in B^* will not be more than 1.75. Next, assume there is no primary replica of class 1 in B^*. In this case, the total size of replicas in B^* is at most $\frac{j+1}{j+\eta}$, and their density is at most $\max\{1.5, (j+\eta)/j\}$, giving them a total weight of at most $\max\{\frac{3j+3}{2j+2\eta}, (j+1)/j\}$, which is at most $\max\{1.5, (j+\eta)/j\} = 1.5$, given that $\eta > 1$ and $j \geq 2$.

Case 3: All Standby Replicas in B^* Are Small: Assume there is no regular standby replica in B^*, but there is at least one small standby replica in B^*. We consider two cases: either there is a primary replica of class 1 in B^* or not:

i) If there is a primary replica y of class 1 in B^*, the remaining space of B^* is less than 1/2 (as y is of size more than 1/2). No other primary replica y' of class 1 can be in B^* because each of y and y' would have a size more than 1/2. Therefore, the remaining space in B^* (of size less than 1/2) can be filled with primary replicas of class $i \geq 2$ (of the density of at most 3/2) and with other standby small replicas (of density 3/2). So, the total weight of items other than y in B^* is at most $1.5(1/2) = 3/4$. Given that the weight of y is 1, the total weight of items in B^* will be at most 1.75.

ii) If there is no primary replica of class 1 in B^*, then B^* is filled with primary replicas of class $i \geq 2$ (of density at most 3/2) and standby replicas of class $j = \lfloor 6\eta \rfloor + 1$ (of the density of 3/2). As a result, the total weight of B^* will be no more than 3/2. □

Theorem 2. HARMONIC-STRETCH *has a competitive ratio of at most 1.75.*

Proof. Let σ be any input sequence, and $w(\sigma)$ be the total weight of items in σ. Let $HS(\sigma)$ be the number of bins that HARMONIC-STRETCH opens for σ. By Lemma 3, we have $HS(\sigma) \leq w(\sigma) + c$ for some constant c independent of $|\sigma|$. On the other hand, by Lemma 4, we have $\text{OPT}(\sigma) \geq w(\sigma)/1.75$. We can write $\frac{HS(\sigma)}{Opt(\sigma)} \leq \frac{w(\sigma)+c}{w(\sigma)/1.75}$, which converges to 1.75, given that c is a constant. □

5 Concluding Remarks

We proved that the competitive ratio of HARMONIC-STRETCH is at most 1.75, which is an improvement over the competitive ratio 2 of the best existing algorithm. We note that this upper bound holds for all values of f and η. When η is close to 1, the existing lower bounds for the classic online bin packing extend to the fault-tolerant setting. In particular, no fault-tolerant bin packing algorithm can achieve a competitive ratio better than 1.54 [3,4]. As a topic for future work, one may consider tightening the gap between the lower bound of 1.54 and the upper bound 1.75.

Acknowledgement. We acknowledge the support of the Natural Sciences and Engineering Research Council of Canada (NSERC).

References

1. Ajiro, Y., Tanaka, A.: Improving packing algorithms for server consolidation. In: Proceedings of the 33rd International Computer Measurement Group Conference (CMG), pp. 399–406 (2007)
2. Azure: Azure virtual machine series. https://azure.microsoft.com/en-ca/
3. Balogh, J., Békési, J., Dósa, G., Epstein, L., Levin, A.: A new lower bound for classic online bin packing. Algorithmica, 1–16 (2021)
4. Balogh, J., Békési, J., Galambos, G.: New lower bounds for certain classes of bin packing algorithms. Theor. Comput. Sci. **440–441**, 1–13 (2012)
5. Daudjee, K., Kamali, S., López-Ortiz, A.: On the online fault-tolerant server consolidation problem. In: Proceedings of the 26th ACM Symposium on Parallelism in Algorithms and Architectures (SPAA), pp. 12–21 (2014)
6. EC2: Amazon EC2 instance types. https://aws.amazon.com/ec2/
7. Lee, C.C., Lee, D.T.: A simple on-line bin-packing algorithm. J. ACM (JACM) **32**(3), 562–572 (1985)
8. Li, B., Dong, Y., Wu, B., Feng, M.: An online fault tolerance server consolidation algorithm. In: Proceedings of the 24th International Conference on Computer Supported Cooperative Work in Design (CSCWD), pp. 458–463 (2021)
9. Li, C., Tang, X.: Towards fault-tolerant bin packing for online cloud resource allocation. In: Proceedings of the 29th ACM Symposium on Parallelism in Algorithms and Architectures (SPAA), pp. 231–233 (2017)
10. Li, C., Tang, X.: On fault-tolerant bin packing for online resource allocation. IEEE Trans. Parallel Distrib. Syst. (TPDS) **31**(4), 817–829 (2020)
11. Mate, J., Daudjee, K., Kamali, S.: Robust multi-tenant server consolidation in the cloud for data analytics workloads. In: Proceedings of the 37th IEEE International Conference on Distributed Computing Systems (ICDCS), pp. 2111–2118 (2017)

12. Ramanan, P., Brown, D.J., Lee, C.C., Lee, D.T.: On-line bin packing in linear time. J. Algorithms **10**(3), 305–326 (1989)
13. Schaffner, J., et al.: RTP: robust tenant placement for elastic in-memory database clusters. In: Proceedings of the 2013 ACM SIGMOD International Conference on Management of Data (SIGMOD), pp. 773–784 (2013)
14. Seiden, S.S.: On the online bin packing problem. J. ACM (JACM) **49**(5), 640–671 (2002)
15. Wu, L., Buyya, R.: Service level agreement (SLA) in utility computing systems. In: Performance and Dependability in Service Computing: Concepts, Techniques and Research Directions, pp. 1–25. IGI Global (2012)
16. Yanagisawa, H., Osogami, T., Raymond, R.: Dependable virtual machine allocation. In: Proceedings of the 32nd IEEE International Conference on Computer Communications (INFOCOM), pp. 629–637 (2013)

R-SWAP: Relay Based Atomic Cross-Chain Swap Protocol

Léonard Lys[1,2,3(✉)], Arthur Micoulet[3], and Maria Potop-Butucaru[1,2]

[1] Sorbonne Université, Paris, France
llys@palo-it.com
[2] LIP6, Paris, France
[3] PALO IT, Paris, France
https://www.palo-it.com/
https://www.lip6.fr/

Abstract. In this paper, we consider the problem of cross-chain transactions where parties that do not trust each other safely exchange digital assets across blockchains. Open blockchains models are decentralized ledgers that keep records of transactions. They are comparable with distributed account books. While they have proven their potential as a store of value, exchanging assets across several blockchains remains a challenge. Our paper proposes a new protocol, R-SWAP, for cross-chain swaps that outperforms existing solutions. Our protocol is built on top of two abstractions: relays and adapters that we formalize for the first time in this paper. Furthermore, we prove the correctness of R-SWAP and analytically evaluate its performances, in terms of cost and latency. Moreover, we evaluate the performances of R-SWAP in two case studies showing the generality of our approach: atomic swaps between Ethereum and Bitcoin (two popular permissionless blockchains) and atomic swaps between Ethereum and Tendermint (one permissionless and one permissioned blockchain).

Keywords: Blockchain · Atomic swap · Cross-chain · Relays

1 Introduction

With the rise of digital assets hosted on blockchain systems came the need for exchanging them across chains. Today, most of the cross-chain exchanges are achieved with the help of a trusted third party, most often an exchange platform. Centralized exchange platforms (CEX's) don't support peer-to-peer cross-chain transactions between users. Instead, users deposit their funds inside the platform's digital wallets and the transactions are handled by the platform's system. Most of the transactions are not even published to the chain. Platforms keep a separate record of their clients assets; the only transactions that are written to the blockchain are deposits and withdraws. This is not a satisfactory solution, because as stated in Bitcoin's white paper [23] all benefits of blockchain technologies are void if a centralized financial institution is required. Indeed, trusting a centralized third party comes with all the flaws of centralization:

© Springer Nature Switzerland AG 2021
G. D'Angelo and O. Michail (Eds.): ALGOCLOUD 2021, LNCS 13084, pp. 18–37, 2021.
https://doi.org/10.1007/978-3-030-93043-1_2

attractive target for attackers [25], governance issues [28], platform commissions, etc. Thus there is a need for solutions that allow users to perform trust-less, cross-chain, peer-to-peer, atomic transactions.

Atomic cross-chain swaps are a solution to this problem. They are distributed protocols where several parties exchange assets across chains. An Atomic cross-chain swap protocol must ensure safety and liveness, i.e., no participant complying with the protocol will lose money and if both participants abide by the protocol, they eventually get their payoffs or get refunded.

In [10], the hash-time locking technique allows participants to exchange assets across chains. But the protocol suffers from a potential violation of safety. In [6,13,26,29] the authors make use of relays for cross-chain payment verification, and hence implement atomic-cross chain swaps. However, those proposals are subject to safety violation because of race condition attacks. Finally in [30] the authors implement Cryptocurrency-backed assets. Those assets emitted on a chain A corresponds to an asset locked on chain B. They make use of relays for cross-chain verification. While this approach shows good performance, strictly speaking, it does not address the problem of cross-chain swap.

Our Contribution. Our contributions are as follows: we propose a new protocol for atomic cross-chain swap, that does not suffer from the limitations of the previous protocols in the literature (e.g. safety violation as in the case of [10] or unfairness issues [29,30]). We propose a formalization and correctness proof of our protocol. We then evaluate analytically its cost and latency. Finally, we evaluate the performances of our protocol considering two case studies: atomic swaps between Bitcoin and Ethereum and atomic swaps between Tendermint and Ethereum. Interestingly, our protocol builds on top of two abstractions that we formalized for the first time: blockchain *relays* and *adapters*. These abstractions can be of independent interest.

Paper Roadmap. Section 2 introduces the system model. In Sect. 3 we propose a formalization for the atomic cross-chain swap, blockchain adapter, and relay abstractions. In Sect. 4 and Sect. 5, we propose a detailed description of our R-SWAP protocol altogether with its correctness proof. Furthermore, in Sect. 6 we analytically evaluate the performances of our protocol. Finally Sect. 7 presents some conclusions and discussions. Due to space limitation additional material is presented in the Appendix.

2 Model and Definitions

2.1 System Model

In this paper, we consider open blockchain systems such as Bitcoin, Ethereum, or Cosmos. Each blockchain system is composed of an arbitrary finite set of processes Π namely $\Pi = \{p_1, p_2, ...\}$. The size of the set Π is not known. However, we assume that at any instant of time there are at most n processes in the system.

Communication. Processes exchange messages through peer-to-peer, bi-directional communication channels. However, as messages can be delayed for an arbitrarily long time we assume asynchronous communication. Each process in the system possesses a pair of public/private keys. Messages are authenticated by digital signature. We consider that it is impossible to forge the signature.

Failure Model. Processes in the system can crash, leave or join at any moment. Moreover we assume processes may exhibit Byzantine behavior [20] (e.g. not relaying messages, delaying them, or broadcasting inconsistent messages). A Byzantine process is said to be *faulty*, otherwise, it is a *correct* process. We assume f faulty processes in the system with $f < n/3$.

2.2 Distributed Ledger Model

A distributed ledger (a.k.a. blockchain) BC is an append-only list of blocks chained together. Each block b_i somehow contains a list of transactions as well as a variable pointing to the previous block b_{i-1}, hence the name blockchain. The blockchain supports two types of operations $\text{READ}(BC)$ and $\text{APPEND}(BC, b_i)$.

Ledger Conflict. This definition only applies to probabilistic delivery blockchains such as Bitcoin. A ledger conflict (or fork) is an event during which two concurrent blocks have been found at the same height h. Due to the system being asynchronous, if two miners find respectively blocks b and b' nearly at the same time, then both b and b' will propagate, resulting in a network partition. A partition P that appended b to their copy of the blockchain and another P' that appended b'.

k-Safety. The parameter k is the depth at which the probability of a fork or ledger conflict is sufficiently low to consider that the risk of this block being abandoned is null. The parameter k depends on the blockchain you are using and the level of safety your system requires. A block that has been appended to the chain and that is now at a depth equal or greater than k. Each new block appended to the chain after the block of interest is called a confirmation. A transaction in a k-valid block is said to be k-valid. It is said to have received k confirmations.

Simple Payment Verification (SPV). Simple payment verification is a process that allows a client to verify the validity of a transaction without having to maintain a full copy of the blockchain. Instead, the client only needs a list of block headers.

Block Time. The block time is the average block creation time. It is calculated by dividing a large period of time by the number of blocks produced during this period. This parameter is specific to each blockchain.

Transaction Validation Time. Let process p broadcast a transaction tx via the primitive $\text{BROADCAST}(<transaction>, tx)$ at time $t_{broadcast}$. Let t_{valid} be the time when the transaction tx appears to be k-valid to p. Then we define the transaction validation time as the difference between t_{valid} and $t_{broadcast}$.

2.3 Asset Model

Blockchain Asset. As of today, blockchain asset refers to anything on the blockchain that serves as a store of value or medium of exchange. It can be coins such as Bitcoins and Ethers, or it can be tokens such as ERC-20 tokens. Nevertheless, blockchain assets share the following properties; A blockchain asset belongs to a public/private key pair. Asset ownership can be transferred through transactions. Asset transfers are recorded to the chain. To transfer the ownership of an asset, one must sign the transaction with the private key.

Asset Locking. An asset on a blockchain is said to be locked when it is not possible to transact it without meeting some conditions. Accessing the said conditions would unlock the asset and allow the user to transact it. Assets are locked thanks to scripts or smart contracts. If the condition to unlock the asset is the expiration of a time-lock, we talk about time locking. If it is the revelation of an hash pre-image, it is hash-locking.

3 Time Locked Atomic Cross-Chain Swap

In this section, we define the time-locked atomic cross-chain swap problem.

3.1 Problem Specification

A time-locked atomic cross-chain swap protocol uses time locking to ensure the termination of the protocol. At the expiration of the time lock, both participants have received an acceptable payoff.

Definition 1 (time-locked atomic cross-chain swap) A time-locked atomic cross-chain swap protocol should satisfy the following properties:

- **Safety.** No participant abiding by the protocol can lose more money than the transaction fees.
- **Time-bounded termination.** No asset can be locked for more than a period of time γ and if an asset is locked, γ is known before locking.
- **Liveness.** Upon lock time expiration, if all participants abided by the protocol and no failures occurred then they received their payoffs.

3.2 Abstractions for Implementing R-SWAP

Blockchain Adapters. A Blockchain adapter is a piece of software that allows sending transactions and query several blockchain systems. In addition to its multiple-blockchain client capabilities, it can perform off-chain computation and storage. It can store private information such as private keys and credentials [19]. A blockchain adapter can be hosted by several instances. The system's goals of a blockchain adapter are:

- Client capabilities: A blockchain adapter should be able to read the state of at least two blockchains, as well as broadcasting transactions.

- Off-chain computation: A blockchain adapter should be able to perform off-chain computations, such as generating a random value and computing its hash.
- Wallet safety: A blockchain adapter should be able to store private credentials and key, without the person running it being able to extract those private data.
- Decentralization: A blockchain adapter should be replicated over several nodes.

Blockchain Relay. A blockchain relay $R_{a \leftarrow b}$ is an abstraction (smart contract or script) on chain BC_a that can receive verification requests of transactions on-chain BC_b. It receives block headers of chain BC_b and performs the standard verification for blocks of BC_b (1). It stores block headers of chain BC_b (2). It can perform Simplified Payment Verification over transactions on-chain BC_b and either returns true if the transaction is valid or false if it is not (3).

Definition 2 (Blockchain Relay) A blockchain relay must satisfy the following properties:

- **k-Validity.** A blockchain relay returns true if the submitted transaction is a k-valid transaction of blockchain BC_b, otherwise it returns false.
- **Eventual Persistent Storage.** Every valid block header of chain BC_b eventually ends up being included in a block appended to BC_a.

A blockchain relay hosted on BC_a that performs verification over blockchain BC_b is noted $R_{a \leftarrow b}$.

Blockchain Relay Latency. We define blockchain relay latency Δ_{relay} as the time difference between the moment a new block b_i is mined on chain BC_b and the moment a verification request for $tx_i \subset b_i$ to the relay $R_{a \leftarrow b}$ with safety parameter k will return true. Let t_{mined} be the time at which a relayer process p of blockchain BC_b delivers a block b_i via the primitive DELIVER. Let t_{valid} be the time when VERIFYTX(tx_i, k) will return true. Then the blockchain relay latency is given by:

$$\Delta_{relay} = t_{valid} - t_{mined} \tag{1}$$

4 R-SWAP Protocol

In this section we detail our R-SWAP protocol and prove its correctness with respect to the time-locked atomic cross-chain swap specification.

4.1 Protocol Overview

The R-SWAP protocol relies on three building blocks; hash time-locked contracts (see Algorithm 2 Appendix C), blockchain relays (Appendix A), and blockchain adapters. Each adapter can send transactions on both blockchain BC_a and BC_b. The unfolding of R-SWAP resembles a hash time-locked contract (HTLC) but it makes use of relays for cross-chain transaction verification and adapters for automation.

In the first phase, participants will commit to the swap by locking their assets with smart contracts. In a second phase, participants will receive their payoffs or refunds (Fig. 1).

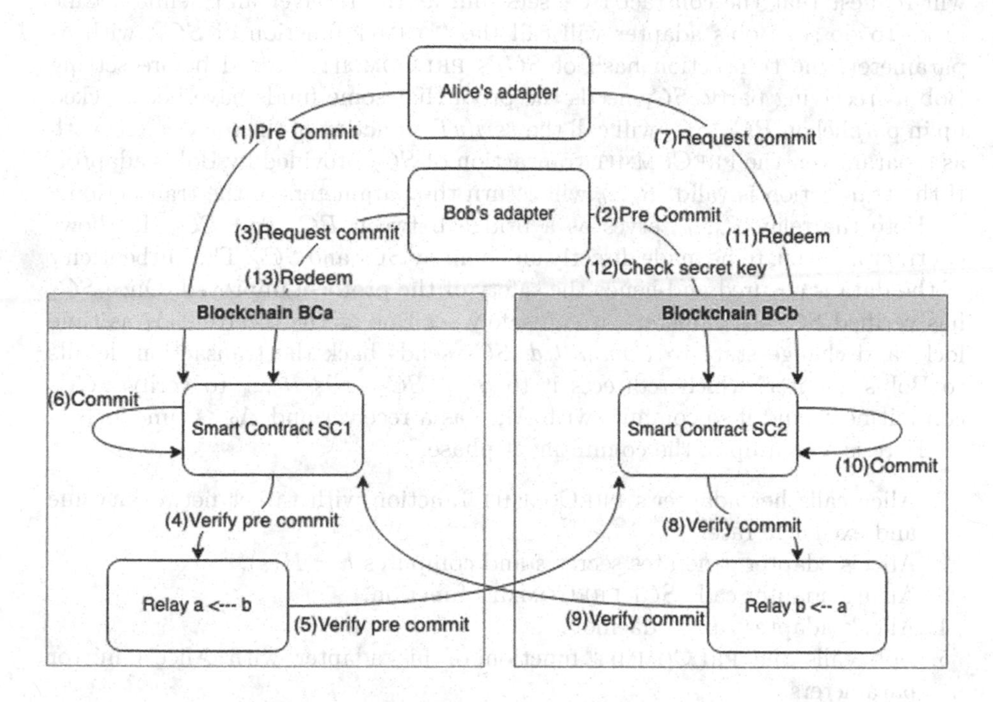

Fig. 1. High level overview of the R-SWAP components and interactions

4.2 Phase 1: Commitment Phase

When Alice wants to execute an atomic cross-chain swap with the R-SWAP protocol, she will request her adapter to lock up funds inside a hash time locked contract SC_1. This contract SC_1 exists in one of five states: *Invalid*, *PreCommitted*, *Committed*, *Redeemed* and *Refunded*. State changes and the corresponding asset transfers are triggered by the following functions: PRECOMMIT, COMMIT, REDEEM, REFUND. State changes are unidirectional. Alice only specifies to the adapter the exchange rate and the amount. The adapter will be responsible for generating a random secret s and computing its hash $h = H(s)$. Then the adapter will lock up the funds inside SC_1 hosted on chain BC_a by calling the PRECOMMIT function.

At this point, the hash lock has been specified, but not the time lock. Hence the assets are not locked, because Alice can ask for a refund at any moment. The PRECOMMIT state serves as proof of ownership.

Bob, a participant interested in the swap, would just have to retrieve the parameters from the chain and request his adaptor to set up a mirror contract SC_2 on blockchain BC_b.

Once the funds are hash locked in SC_2 trough PRECOMMIT function, Bob will request that the contract SC_1 sets him as the receiver and define a time lock. To do so, Bob's adapter will call the COMMIT function of SC_1, with as parameter, the transaction hash of SC_2's PRECOMMIT. Indeed before setting Bob as receiving party, SC_1 needs the proof that some funds have been locked up in parallel on BC_b. SC_1 will call the *verifyTx* function of the relay $R_{a \leftarrow b}$, with as a parameter, the PRECOMMIT transaction of SC_2 provided by Bob's adaptor. If the transaction is valid, $R_{a \leftarrow b}$ will return the parameters of the transaction.

Here the relay $R_{a \leftarrow b}$ serves as a bridge between BC_a and BC_b. It allows contract auditing to be made directly on-chain by SC_1 and SC_2. The authenticity of the data is ensured and hence the safety of the protocol improved. Once SC_1 has verified SC_2's parameters, it can safely set Bob as the receiver, Δ_1 as time lock, and change state to *Committed*. SC_1 sends back the transaction details to Bob's adapter, which redirects it to SC_2. SC_2 calls $R_{b \leftarrow a}$ to verify SC_1's commitment, and if so commits with Alice as a receiver and Δ_2 as time lock.

Here is a sum-up of the commitment phase.

1. Alice calls her adapter's PRECOMMIT function with target network, value and exchange rate.
2. Alice's adapter generates secret s and computes $h = H(s)$.
3. Alice's adapter calls SC_1 PRECOMMIT function.
4. Alice's adapter runs a daemon.
5. Bob calls the PRECOMMIT function of his adapter with Alice's mirror parameters.
6. Bob's adapter calls SC_2 PRECOMMIT function.
7. Bob's adapter calls SC_1 COMMIT function.
8. SC_1 calls the relay $R_{a \leftarrow b}$ to verify that SC_2 is in state *PreCommitted.*
9. On receiving the proof that SC_2 is in state *PreCommitted* SC_1 changes its state to *Committed* sets Bob as receiver and Δ_1 as time lock.
10. On receiving proof that SC_1 is *Committed*, Bob's adapter calls SC_2 COMMIT function.
11. SC_2 calls the relay $R_{b \leftarrow a}$ to verify that SC_1 is in *Committed* state.
12. On receiving the proof that SC_1 is on *Committed* state, SC_2 changes its state to *Committed* sets Alice as receiver and Δ_2 as time lock.
13. Bob's adapter runs a daemon.

4.3 Phase 2: Contracts Redeem/Refund

Daemon. At stage 4 and 13 each adapters have run a daemon. Those daemons are awaiting a state change of SC_2 before they move on to the redeem/refund phase. For each new block of BC_b Alice's daemon will check if Bob's contract SC_2 has changed from state *PreCommitted* to *Committed*. This would mean that Bob has committed to the swap and thus that she can move on to the redeem phase. For each new block of the blockchain, BC_b Bob's daemon will check if SC_2 has changed from state *Committed* to *Redeemed*. This would mean that Alice has redeemed, and by doing so, revealed the secret key. Bob can now move on to the redeem phase.

Those daemons also handle the cases where some party would stop abiding by the protocol. They have stored the time lock values and a REFUND transaction call is scheduled at the expiration of the time lock.

Here is a sum-up of the second phase, if participants abide by the protocol:

1. Alice's adapter calls SC_1 CHECKSTATE function
2. If state is *Committed* call SC_2 CHECKSTATE function
3. If state is *Committed* Alice's adapter calls REDEEM function of SC_2 with s, triggering the asset transfer to her address
4. Bob's adapter calls SC_2 CHECKSECRETKEY function
5. If key is revealed Bob's adapter calls SC_1's REDEEM function with the secret s he just learned, triggering the asset transfer to his address.

If one of the participants does not abide by the protocol, the daemon will simply call REFUND at the expiration of their respective smart contract's time lock expiration.

5 R-SWAP Correctness

In this section, we prove the correctness of the protocol, i.e., that it satisfies the properties of safety, time-bounded termination, and liveness of a time-locked atomic cross-chain swap, defined in Sect. 3.1. Due to space limitation the time lock values determination for our R-SWAP protocol is discussed in Appendix B.

Lemma 1. *R-SWAP protocol satisfies the time-bounded termination property of a time-locked atomic cross-chain swap.*

Proof. In the following we prove that there exists a bounded value $\gamma > 0$ such that the R-SWAP protocol verifies the time-bounded termination property with parameter γ. Suppose R-SWAP protocol violates the time-bounded termination property. A violation of the time-bounded termination property implies that an asset is locked forever, thus excluding all set of states before *PreCommitted/PreCommitted*, *PreCommitted/PreCommitted* included. Indeed, before being in the state *Committed*, contracts are only hash-locked, not time-locked and thus can be refunded. Given the possible set of states, subsequent possible states are *Committed/PreCommitted*, *PreCommitted/Refunded* and *Refunded/PreCommitted*. *PreCommitted/Refunded* and *Refunded/PreCommitted* don't imply a violation of the time-bounded termination property since assets are refunded or can be refunded, so the only case to consider is the set *Committed/PreCommitted*.

To transition to this set, SC_1 must commit. It does so by calling the COMMIT function with as a parameter Δ_1. Δ_1's value is hardcoded in the contract (see Appendix B), thus it is known and finite. The result of the SC_1's commitment is a transaction tx.

Subsequently, three sets of state are possible:

- *Refunded/PreCommitted*: Since Δ_1 is known and finite, SC_1 will eventually be able to move to $Refunded$, not leading to a violation of the time bounded termination property. In this case the asset cannot be locked for more than $\gamma = \Delta_1 + \lambda_a$.
- *Committed/Committed*: To proceed to state *Committed*, SC_2 calls $R_{b \leftarrow a}$ to verify tx. If the relay returns true then SC_2 extracts Δ_1 from tx. It then proceeds to call it's own COMMIT function with as a parameter $\Delta_2 = \lambda_b$ (see Appendix B). Yet a violation of the time bounded termination property would imply that the time lock value was unknown, leading to a contradiction.
- *Committed/Refunded*: Since its asset was not locked, SC_2 can be refunded. But since Δ_1 is known and finite, $SC1$ will eventually be able to move to $Refunded$, not leading to a violation of the time-bounded termination property.

Out of those three sets of states, the only one of interest is *Committed/Committed*, as the other two involve SC_1 being able to call REFUND. Since Δ_1 is known and bounded, SC_1 will be able to call REFUND at the expiration of Δ_1. Thus, from now on, the potential violation of the time-bounded termination property only concerns SC_2. From the set of state *Committed/Committed* two set of states are possible:

- *Committed/Redeemed*: Since Bob has extracted h from Alice's COMMIT transaction tx, she can call the REDEEM function of SC_2 with the secret s. By doing so she triggers the asset transfer from SC_2 to her address. As she has revealed s to Bob, if Bob's adapter is correct it will automatically call the REDEEM function of SC_1, triggering the asset transfer from SC_1 to Bob's address. Since the transaction has a high probability of being included prior to Δ_2's expiration, the protocol satisfies the time bounded termination property.
- *Refunded/Committed*: If Alice has been refunded, it means that Δ_1 has expired. If Bob's adapter is correct, it would have called the REFUND function of SC_2 right after the publication of the block containing Alice's refund transaction. Since $\Delta_1 \geq \Delta_2 + \Delta_{relay}$, Bob's REFUND transaction will be included with a high probability, leading to a contradiction.

Overall, an asset can remain locked at most $\gamma = \max(\Delta_1 + \lambda_a, \Delta_1 + \lambda_a)$ time. Thus the R-SWAP protocol satisfies the time-bounded termination property with parameter γ.

Lemma 2. *The R-SWAP protocol satisfies the safety property of a time-locked atomic cross-chain swap.*

Proof. Assume R-SWAP protocol violates the safety property of the time-locked atomic cross-chain swap specification. This safety violation implies that there exist two smart contracts SC_1 and SC_2 one being in state *Redeemed* and the other *Refunded.* Indeed, any other set of state is impossible or doesn't imply a safety violation. We also exclude the case of an asset being locked forever because of the time-bounded termination property.

SC_1 being redeemed and SC_2 refunded, imply that Bob has found the secret s because SC_1 is programmed to change state to redeemed only if provided s. This leads to a contradiction because it is impossible to calculate s from h.

SC_1 being redeemed and SC_2 being refunded imply that Alice has called the redeem function of SC_2. By doing so she has revealed the secret s. But given that the adapter checks the state of SC_2 at every new block, and given that the block time is $<< \Delta_2$ (see Appendix B), at the time Alice will be allowed to call refund, SC_1 will already be in state *Redeemed,* leading to a contradiction.

Lemma 3. *The R-SWAP protocol satisfies the liveness property of the time-locked atomic cross-chain swap problem with high probability.*

Proof. Assume R-SWAP protocol violates the liveness property of the time-locked atomic cross-chain swap problem. A violation of the liveness property implies that upon lock time expiration both contracts are in state *Redeemed* but one or more of the participants have not received their payoffs. Since SC_1 and SC_2 are programmed to transfer the assets before the transition to state *Redeemed,* a violation of the liveness property implies that the receiver address provided during the commit transaction $tx1_{com}$ of SC_1 resp. $tx2_{com}$ of SC_2 was not Bob resp. Alice.

When calling SC_1 COMMIT function, Bob's adapter has provided the details of the PRECOMMIT transaction $tx2_{pre}$ of SC_2. Then the COMMIT function of SC_1 has called $R_{a \leftarrow b}$ to verify $tx2_{pre}$. If the transaction is valid, SC_1 proceed to extract Bob's address from $tx2_{pre}$, set him as receiver and changes its state to *Committed.* Yet a violation of the liveness property would suppose that this address was something else, leading to a contradiction.

SC_2 COMMIT function works the same way, but instead of providing the PRE-COMMIT transaction, Alice's adapter provides the COMMIT transaction details $tx1_{com}$. Prior to committing, SC_2 calls $R_{b \leftarrow a}$ to verify $tx1_{com}$. If it was a valid transaction, SC_2 extracts Alice's address from $tx1_{com}$ and calls its own COMMIT function with the address previously extracted as a parameter. Yet a violation of the liveness property would suppose that the address provided was something else, leading to a contradiction.

Note on Non-deterministic Blockchains. It should be noted that in proof-of-work blockchain systems such as Bitcoin and Ethereum, block creation is probabilistic. However it is proven in [9] that under the assumption of an honest majority of nodes $t \leq \frac{1-\delta}{2}(n-t)$, Bitcoin satisfies agreement and validity properties with probability at least $1 - e^{-\Omega(\epsilon^2 \lambda f)}$ with n number of parties mining; t out of which are controlled by the adversary, δ the advantage of honest parties, ϵ

the quality of concentration of random variables in typical executions, λ the tail-bounds parameter and f the probability at least one honest party succeeds in finding a POW in a round. Thus, for such blockchain systems, R-SWAP satisfies the properties of a time-locked atomic cross-chain swap with high probability.

6 R-SWAP Evaluation

In this section, we will analytically evaluate the performances of the R-SWAP protocol. A numerical projection and cost analysis is given in the Appendix D.

There is no reliable global clock in most blockchain systems thus latency can only be measured from the participants' blockchain client's perspective.

Definition 3 (Atomic Swap Latency) Let *Locked*, *Refund* and *Redeem* be three predicates. Let p be a participant in an atomic cross-chain swap. Predicate $Locked = true$ indicates that p's asset is locked. Predicate $Refund = true$ indicates that p has received his refund and can transact it. Predicate $Redeem = true$ indicates that p has received his payoff and can transact it. Let t_l be the time when $Locked = true$. Let t_u be the time when $Refund \vee Redeem = true$. Then the atomic swap latency is defined by:

$$\Delta_{latency} = t_u - t_l \qquad (2)$$

In the following, we theoretically analyze the latency of the R-SWAP protocol. Numerical analysis is in Appendix D.

Let λ be the upper bound on transaction validation and let Δ be the time lock value of a R-SWAP contract SC. As proven in Sect. 5, the R-SWAP protocol is time-bounded. In the case every participant is honest and abide by the protocol, the atomic swap latency of the R-SWAP protocol is less than Δ_1, the lock time of contract SC_1. In the case Bob stopped abiding by the protocol after Alice's COMMIT transaction, she will have to wait for Δ_1's expiration before calling REFUND. Then this REFUND transaction will be confirmed in less than λ_a, the transaction validation time of blockchain BC_a. From Alice's point of view, this is a latency of less than $\Delta_1 + \lambda_a$. In the case Alice stopped abiding by the protocol after Bob's COMMIT transaction, he will have to wait for the expiration of Δ_2 before calling REFUND on SC_2. This gives a latency of $\Delta_2 + \lambda_b$ for Bob and $\Delta_1 + \lambda_a$ for Alice. Thus the overall maximum latency is $\Delta_{lantency} = 3\lambda_b + \lambda_a$.

Case \ Max latency	Alice	Bob
Alice & Bob abide by the protocol	Δ_1	Δ_1
Bob stops after Alice's Commit	$\Delta_1 + \lambda_a$	None
Alice stops after Bob's Commit	$\Delta_1 + \lambda_a$	$\Delta_2 + \lambda_b$

Fig. 2. Table of R-SWAP theoretical latency

7 Conclusions and Discussions

This paper presents R-SWAP, a time-bounded atomic cross-chain swap protocol that makes use of blockchain relays and adapters to address the shortcomings of the hash locking technique. Previously proposed atomic cross-chain swap protocols such as [10] were subject to a potential safety violation. Indeed, the safety of such protocols could only be satisfied with the assumption that no errors occurred on the participant's blockchain client. Moreover, the smart contract auditing tasks were to be executed by the participants, leading to bad ergonomics and potential safety violations. The R-SWAP protocol makes use of blockchain relay $R_{a \leftarrow b}$ to verify transactions of chain BC_b from chain BC_a thus automating the contract auditing process. The protocol also involves distributed blockchain APIs, namely blockchain adapters that reduce the risks of a client crash compromising the swap's safety.

We formally prove that the R-SWAP protocol satisfies the properties of a time-bounded atomic cross-chain swap with a maximum latency $\Delta_{latency} = 3\lambda_b + \lambda_a$, where λ's represents a specific blockchain's upper bound on transaction validation time.

The operational cost of the infrastructure required for the R-SWAP protocol can be narrowed down to the cost of the relay. Indeed the blockchain relay is undoubtedly the piece of software that has the highest operational cost, as high as 3600$ per day for a Bitcoin relay on the Ethereum blockchain at the current price. However recent research [8] suggests that the operational cost of relays could be reduced by 92%.

A Blockchain Relay Smart Contract Class

Algorithm 1. Blockchain Relay smart contract class

```
1: bytes [] blocks                                 ▷ Table to store block headers
2: procedure STOREBLOCKHEADER(blockHeader)
3:     requires(VALIDATEPOW(blockHeader))
4:     THIS.BLOCKS.APPEND(blockHeader)             ▷ If the block is valid, store block
5: end procedure
6: procedure VERIFYTX(tx, k)
7:     return VALIDATESPV(tx.txid, tx.root, tx.proof, tx.index, k)
8: end procedure
```

Protocol A is a possible interface for a blockchain relay. It presents the main functions of such software. The function VALIDATEPOW (line 3) implements the Proof of Work verification protocol of the relayed blockchain. It returns true if the provided block header is valid and false otherwise. The function VALIDATESPV (line 7) implements the simple payment verification of provided transaction.

It returns true if it is a valid transaction and false otherwise. The parameter k in function VERIFYTX(tx, k) is the safety factor. It specifies at what height the block containing the transaction tx must be in the relay's data store to consider the transaction as valid. Complete implementation of VALIDATEPoW and VALIDATESPV can be found in [11].

B Time Lock Value Determination

Choosing the right value for the time locks is essential. A time lock value that is too short could lead to a safety violation. Conversely, a time lock value that is too long could be commercially unfair, as prices are very volatile.

Consider a swap executed via the relays swap protocol. The swap is executed between blockchains BC_a and BC_b. k_a resp. k_b is the k parameter of BC_a resp. BC_b (see k-safety in Sect. 2.2). ζ_a is the target block time of BC_a and ζ_b of BC_b. There are two time locks values to be chosen; Δ_1 for SC_1 and Δ_2 for SC_2.

The first value of interest is the difference between Δ_1 and Δ_2. This difference has to be long enough for the participant to call the redeem function and for this transaction to be included in a valid block. If not long enough this could lead to a safety violation. Δ_1 and Δ_2 are strongly dependent on parameters specific to each blockchain. A naive estimation of the minimal value for the difference between time locks could be:

$$\Delta_1 - \Delta_2 = (\zeta_b k_b) \tag{3}$$

Assuming synchronous communication, this should be long enough for the redeem transaction to be included in a valid block. But as stated in the model, the block time is not necessarily fixed and blocks can be delayed for an arbitrarily long time, leading to potential safety violations.

Therefore for the rest of this paper, we will assume that there is a time λ, specific to each blockchain, within which a broadcast transaction will be included in a block and receive k confirmations with a probability ϵ. Thus $\Delta_1 - \Delta_2 \geq \lambda_b$ is the first constraint to satisfy the safety property, where λ_b is the upper bound on transaction validation for blockchain BC_b.

The second constraint does not concern safety, but commercial fairness. Bob will not call the COMMIT function of SC_2 unless he is sure that SC_1 is *Committed.* He needs the guarantee that Alice's commitment is a valid transaction. If it is not yet, in the fear of a safety violation, Bob should choose not to COMMIT and instead call REFUND on SC_2. Alice would end up having her assets locked for at least λ_b, which is commercially unfair for her. Thus, for the swap to be fair, time-locks should be chosen such that $\Delta_1 \geq \Delta_2 + \lambda_a$.

We obtain the following:

$$\Delta_1 \geq \Delta_2 + max\{\lambda_a, \lambda_b\} \tag{4}$$

Now that we found the minimal value for Δ_1, we want to find a minimal value for Δ_2. We want to minimize the duration of the swap for commercial fairness. If

$\Delta_2 = 0$, Bob can call for a REFUND on SC_2 at any moment. Yet he cannot ask for REDEEM on SC_1 either he doesn't know s. Alice's adapter has been triggered by Bob's COMMIT and proceeds to call REDEEM on SC_2. This REDEEM transaction contains s in plain text as a parameter. At this point this redeem transaction is not confirmed yet, but still waiting in the mempool. As transactions are public, Bob can run a transaction sniffer that would extract s from Alice's unconfirmed REDEEM transaction. Then he would send two transaction: REFUND on SC_2 and REDEEM on SC_1 with the secret s he just sniffed, leading to a safety violation. He could even increase its chances of success by setting high transaction fees.

Therefore it is necessary that Δ_2 be long enough for Alice to call REDEEM on SC_2 and for this transaction to be included in a valid block. Thus we have:

$$\Delta_2 \geq \lambda_b \tag{5}$$

Relay Latency. Cross chain transaction verification requires that, for each new block b_i produced on chain BC_b, a relayer submits b_i to the relay $R_{a\leftarrow b}$. Thus, between the time a block b_i is produced on chain BC_b and the time VERIFYTX(tx), $tx \subset b_i$ to the relay $R_{a\leftarrow b}$ will return true, there is a maximum delay given by [30].

$$\Delta_{relay} = \lambda_b + \Delta_{submit} + 2\lambda_a \tag{6}$$

λ_a and λ_b being the upper bound on transaction validation time of blockchain BC_a resp. BC_b. Δ_{submit} is the delay between the moment a block is produced and the moment a relayer submits the block to the relay.

In the R-SWAP protocol, each relay $R_{a\leftarrow b}$ and $R_{b\leftarrow a}$ is called once. SC_1 calls VERIFYTX(tx, k) at stage 8 to verify that SC_2 is in state *PreCommitted*. SC_2 calls the relay $R_{b\leftarrow a}$ at stage 11 to verify that SC_1 is in state *Committed*.

Let $tx1_{com}$ be the commitment transaction of SC_1. There is a latency Δ_{relay} during which the relay $R_{b\leftarrow a}$ will not consider $tx1_{com}$ as a valid transaction. Thus calling VERIFYTX($tx1_{com}, k$) on $R_{b\leftarrow a}$ during this period of time might return false. Thus the time lock value Δ_1 of contract SC_1, must be such that $\Delta_1 \geq \Delta_{relay}$. Considering relay's delay we must now ensure that Δ_1 is large enough for the commit transaction of SC_1 to be valid regarding the relay:

$$\Delta_1 \geq \Delta_2 + \Delta_{relay} \tag{7}$$

or

$$\Delta_1 \geq \Delta_2 + \lambda_a + \Delta_{submit} + 2\lambda_b \tag{8}$$

Finally we obtain the following system of inequalities for the time lock values:

$$\begin{cases} \Delta_1 \geq \Delta_2 + \lambda_a + \Delta_{submit} + 2\lambda_b \\ \Delta_2 \geq \lambda_b \end{cases} \tag{9}$$

C R-SWAP Smart Contract

msg is a variable generated when executing a transaction. It contains several information relative to the transaction such as the address of the function caller *msg.sender* or the value of the transaction *msg.value*. Smart contract is presented in Algorithm 2.

Algorithm 2. R-SWAP hash time lock contract class

```
1: address sender;                                      ▷ Address of swap initiator
2: address receiver;                                    ▷ Address of participant
3: float amount;                                        ▷ Amount exchanged
4: float rate;                                          ▷ Exchange rate
5: integer timelock;
6: bytes secret;
7: bytes hashLock;                                      ▷ Hash of the secret
8: address Relay;                                       ▷ Address of the relay smart contract
9: enum State{Invalid, PreCommitted, Committed, Redeemed, Refunded}
10: State state ← Invalid                               ▷ Variable to store state
11: procedure PRECOMMIT(hashLock, amount, rate)
12:     requires(this.state = Invalid)
13:     this.hashLock ← hashLock
14:     this.amount ← amount
15:     this.rate ← rate
16:     this.sender ← msg.sender
17:     this.state ← PreCommitted
18: end procedure
19: procedure COMMIT(tx)
20:     requires(this.state = PreCommitted)
21:     requires(RELAY.VERIFYTX(tx)) ▷ Calling the relay to verify that the provided
    transaction is valid
22:     requires(tx.hashLock = this.hashLock)           ▷ Verifying the hash lock
23:     requires(tx.amount = this.amount * this.rate)   ▷ Verifying the amount
24:     this.receiver ← msg.sender                      ▷ Setting the function caller as receiver
25:     this.timelock ← now + Δ1                        ▷ Setting up the time lock
26:     this.state ← Committed
27: end procedure
28: procedure REDEEM(secret)
29:     requires(this.state = Committed)
30:     requires(msg.sender = this.receiver)            ▷ Check that the caller is the swap
    receiver
31:     requires(SHA256(secret)= this.hashLock)         ▷ Verify the secret
32:     this.secret ← secret                            ▷ Make the secret public
33:     TRANSFER(this.amount, this.receiver)            ▷ Transfer the funds
34:     this.state ← Redeemed
35: end procedure
36: procedure REFUND
37:     requires(this.state ≠ Redeemed)
38:     requires(msg.sender = this.sender) ▷ Verify that the caller is the swap sender
39:     requires(this.timelock ≥ now)                   ▷ Check that timelock is elapsed
40:     TRANSFER(this.amount, this.sender)              ▷ Transfer the funds
41:     this.state ← Refunded
42: end procedure
43: procedure CHECKSTATE
44:     return this.state
45: end procedure
46: procedure CHECKSECRETKEY
47:     return this.secret
48: end procedure
```

D Numerical Analysis of R-SWAP Latency

The value of the latency is highly dependant on the set of blockchain involved in the swap because time locks are based on the upper bound of transaction validation time λ with probability ϵ, which is specific to each blockchain. In this section we will provide a numerical analysis of the swap latency between the two most valued cryptocurrencies in terms of market cap at the time of writing: Bitcoin and Ethereum [5].

Bitcoin's Upper Bound on Transaction Validation Time. Calculating Bitcoin's or any blockchain's upper bound on transaction validation time is a very complex problem. Indeed, it depends on numerous factors such as transaction fees, network traffic, current hash rate and difficulty, size of the unconfirmed transaction mempool, etc. But it has been shown in [14] that the main factors are transaction fee density (in satoshi/Byte) and network traffic.

It is known that miners order transactions in their mempool by fee density to maximize profitability [12]. By setting sufficiently high fee density it is possible to predict that a transaction will be included in the next block with a probability p as high as 95% [16]. Then to find an estimation of Bitcoin's upper bound on transaction validation time, we must ensure that once the transaction has been included, there is enough time for $k = 6$ new blocks to be appended to the chain, i.e., to receive $k = 6$ confirmations. Block time in Bitcoin follows an exponential distribution with parameter $\theta = 0.001578$ [7]. Thus the probability of k blocks being mined in less than x time is given by the PDF of the gamma distribution Gamma(k,θ) cumulative function.

As most blockchain clients consider $k = 6$ being a safe number of confirmations we obtain the value of Fig. 3.

$P(X < x)$	x (in seconds)
0.95	6662.25
0.99	8307.02
0.995	8966.89
0.999	10427.60

Fig. 3. Probability for 6 blocks to be mined in less than x seconds

Thus with a fee density high enough for the transaction to be included in the next block with high probability $p = 0.95$, there is an upper bound on this transaction validation time $\lambda_{btc} = 10427\,\text{s}$ with high probability.[1] Rounded up, this translates to a 3 h validation time.

[1] $p = 0.95 * 0.999 = 0.949$. It is to be noted that even if the transaction has not received 6 confirmations yet, it should have received at least 5 confirmation with probability >0.949, and should receive its 6th confirmation in the next ten minutes.

Ethereum's Upper Bound on Transaction Validation Time. A study based on the Ethereum blockchain data [22] showed that 99% of the blocks were produced in less than a minute. Thus with $k = 12$, twelve minutes after its inclusion in a block, a transaction should be k-valid with a high probability $p \approx 1$. Therefore with sufficient gas price, there is an upper bound on transaction validation time for Ethereum $\lambda_{eth} = (k * 60) + 30 = 750$ s with high probability.[2]

Latency for a Swap Between Bitcoin and Ethereum. Consider an R-SWAP protocol execution between Bob and Alice. Alice, the initiator, has bitcoins. Bob, the participant, has ethers. (The initiator is the one that generates the secret). Given the values of upper bounds on transaction validation time, given the theoretical latency values of Fig. 2 and given the values of time locks of Sect. B, the estimation of the maximum latency values for this swap are presented in Fig. 4a. (We selected $\Delta_{btc} = 8307$ s and $\Delta_{eth} = 750$ s).

Case \ Max latency	Alice	Bob
All abide	10 557	10 557
Bob stops	18 864	n.a
Alice stops	18 864	1500

(a) Latency for a R-SWAP execution between Bitcoin and Ethereum

Case \ Max latency	Alice	Bob
All abide	771	771
Bob stops	1521	n.a
Alice stops	1521	14

(b) Latency for a R-SWAP execution between Ethereum and Tendermint

Fig. 4. Latency of the R-SWAP protocol

Tendermint Upper Bound on Transaction Validation Time. Block-chain systems such as Cosmos [15] uses the Tendermint Byzantine fault tolerant (BFT) consensus [4]. Tendermint BFT consensus satisfies the instant finality property. With our model, this translates to having a safety factor $k = 1$. Thus, the Tendermint upper bound on transaction validation time is nothing else than the Tendermint block time. As of today, the observed block time is seven seconds [18]. Thus for Tendermint we have $\lambda_{tendermint} = 7$.

Latency for a Swap Between Tendermint and Ethereum. Consider an R-SWAP protocol execution between Tendermint and Ethereum. The initiator (the one generating the hash lock) has ethers and the participant has atoms (Cosmos native asset). For such a swap we obtain the latency values presented in Fig. 4b. Cosmos recently launched the Stargate update [2] which allows cross-chain transactions. The inter blockchain communication protocol used to achieve cross-chain transactions uses some sort of pegging like X-Claim [30]. As this is a work in progress, we do not have a performance evaluation of this protocol.

[2] This is a 12 min and 30 s total validation time.

E Cost Evaluation

In this section, we will analyze the operational cost of the infrastructure required to implement the R-SWAP protocol. The R-SWAP protocol is made out of three software bricks; hash time-locked contracts, blockchain adapters, and relays. Operating an external adapter is as costly as operating a blockchain node. A single hash time-locked contract can be used for a large number of swaps, making the deployment cost negligible. Thus the operational costs of the infrastructure narrow down to the cost of operating the relays.

Operational Cost of Relays. As explained in Sect. 3.2, a relay $R_{a \leftarrow b}$ is a piece of software, possibly a smart contract, that allows to read and verify the state of chain BC_b from chain BC_a [31]. The intuition is that a relayer r publishes every new block header of chain BC_b to the relay $R_{a \leftarrow b}$ on chain BC_a. The relay implements the block verification protocol of chain BC_b. It verifies the proof of work for PoW chains or the signature of 2/3 of the validators for BFT consensus chains [8]. Then, once the block has been verified, a process can call the relay to verify a specific transaction of chain BC_b from BC_a. He pays a little fee that will compensate the relayer's work and expenses. Depending on the blockchain, this process can be both calculation and storage-intensive. Unfortunately, storage and calculation "on-chain" is expensive in most blockchain systems, inevitably leading to high operational costs. Current implementation such as BTCRelay [6] used about 194 000 gas to store and verify a single Bitcoin block header[3]. Gas price and ether price are subject to high volatility. Thus it is important to note that what follows can vary from one day to another but to give a rough estimate, as of today's prices[4], this would translate to 25$ per relayed block. Considering that an average of 144 Bitcoin blocks are mined every day, maintaining the BTCRelay would cost alone about 3600$/day. If the volume of R-SWAP transactions is large enough, those operational costs could be amortized by an economy of scale, each swap participant paying a small fee to the relayer. The other outlays concerning the relays is the computational power required to verify a submitted transaction. For each R-SWAP execution, each participant request at least one transaction verification to the relay. On modern implementation of BTCRealy, the cost of such an operation vary from 67000 to 102000 gas [11].

As of today, the operating cost of the relay is quite dissuasive, especially considering that current centralized exchange platforms offer fees as low as 0.1%[5]. Fortunately, recent research suggests that the operational cost of blockchain relays could be reduced by up to 92% [8], thanks to an "on-demand" approach.

F Other Related Works

There are currently several operational systems for achieving interoperability between different blockchains (e.g. Cosmos [15] or Polkadot [27]). However, they

[3] https://etherscan.io/address/0x41f274c0023f83391de4e0733c609df5a124c3d4.
[4] eth price: 1293$, gas price: 100Gwei.
[5] https://www.binance.com/en/fee/schedule.

are not yet fully formalized and proved correct. Moreover, there is no academic study focusing on their performances.

The first atomic swap was proposed for Bitcoin by Nolan [17]. This solution uses hash-time locked contracts enabling conditional asset transfers. In [10] the authors generalize Nolan's scheme and propose its analyses using a game-theoretical approach. This analysis has been refined later in [1]. Other projects such as BartherDEX [24], part of the Komodo project [21], represents a cross-chain solution that matches orders and defines the swap protocol or Blockchain.io [3] implements atomic cross-chain swaps by combining centralized components (order matching) with decentralized ones (trade settlement and execution). These projects are not yet formally proved correct.

The academic research focuses on hybrid swap protocols, replacing decentralized commitment/locking schemes (hash-locks) with centralized ones, resulting in more attractive and efficient protocols. AC3TW and AC3WN [29] protocols propose atomic cross-chain swaps respectively with centralized and distributed trusted authorities (i.e., witnesses).

References

1. Belotti, M., Moretti, S., Potop-Butucaru, M., Secci, S.: Game theoretical analysis of atomic cross-chain swaps. In: 40th IEEE International Conference on Distributed Computing Systems (ICDCS) (2020)
2. Birch, G.: Cosmos stargate update overview (2020). https://figment.io/resources/cosmos-stargate-upgrade-overview/#ibc
3. Blockchain.io: Blockchain.io your gateway to the internet of value. https://blockchain.io/
4. Braithwaite, S., et al.: Tendermint blockchain synchronization: formal specification and model checking. In: Margaria, T., Steffen, B. (eds.) ISoLA 2020. LNCS, vol. 12476, pp. 471–488. Springer, Cham (2020). https://doi.org/10.1007/978-3-030-61362-4_27
5. CoinMarketCap: Cryptocurrency prices, charts and market capitalizations. https://coinmarketcap.com/
6. Consensys: ethereum/btcrelay, October 2017. https://github.com/ethereum/btcrelay
7. Decker, C., Wattenhofer, R.: Information propagation in the bitcoin network. In: IEEE P2P 2013 Proceedings, pp. 1–10 (2013). https://doi.org/10.1109/P2P.2013.6688704
8. Frauenthaler, P., Sigwart, M., Spanring, C., Schulte, S.: Testimonium: a cost-efficient blockchain relay. arXiv preprint arXiv:2002.12837 (2020)
9. Garay, J., Kiayias, A., Leonardos, N.: The bitcoin backbone protocol: analysis and applications. In: Oswald, E., Fischlin, M. (eds.) EUROCRYPT 2015. LNCS, vol. 9057, pp. 281–310. Springer, Heidelberg (2015). https://doi.org/10.1007/978-3-662-46803-6_10
10. Herlihy, M.: Atomic cross-chain swaps. In: Proceedings of the 2018 ACM Symposium on Principles of Distributed Computing, PODC 2018, pp. 245–254. Association for Computing Machinery, New York (2018). https://doi.org/10.1145/3212734.3212736

11. Interlay: interlay/btc-relay-solidity (2020). https://github.com/interlay/BTC-Relay-Solidity
12. Kasahara, S., Kawahara, J.: Effect of bitcoin fee on transaction-confirmation process. arXiv preprint arXiv:1604.00103 (2016)
13. Kiayias, A., Zindros, D.: Proof-of-work sidechains. In: Bracciali, A., Clark, J., Pintore, F., Rønne, P.B., Sala, M. (eds.) FC 2019. LNCS, vol. 11599, pp. 21–34. Springer, Cham (2020). https://doi.org/10.1007/978-3-030-43725-1_3
14. Koops, D.: Predicting the confirmation time of bitcoin transactions. arXiv preprint arXiv:1809.10596 (2018)
15. Kwon, J., Buchman, E.: Cosmos: a network of distributed ledgers (2016). https://cosmos.network/whitepaper
16. Newbery, J.: An introduction to bitcoin core fee estimation, October 2018. https://bitcointechtalk.com/an-introduction-to-bitcoin-core-fee-estimation-27920880ad0
17. Nolan, T.: Alt chains and atomic transfers (2013). https://bitcointalk.org/index.php?topic=193281.msg2224949#msg2224949
18. Omar, F.: Cosmos network now has nearly 100 validators, 6–7 second block times, April 2019. https://www.cryptoglobe.com/latest/2019/04/cosmos-network-now-has-nearly-100-validators-6-7-second-block-times/
19. Patrick, C.: Building and using external adapters, January 2021. https://blog.chain.link/build-and-use-external-adapters/
20. Pease, M., Shostak, R., Lamport, L.: Reaching agreement in the presence of faults. J. ACM **27**(2), 228–234 (1980)
21. Platform, K.: Komodo, an advanced blockchain technology, focused on freedom, June 2018. https://static2.coinpaprika.com/storage/cdn/whitepapers/140811.pdf
22. Rolandkofler: rolandkofler/blocktime (2017). https://github.com/rolandkofler/blocktime
23. Satoshi, N.: Bitcoin: a peer-to-peer electronic cash system. Technical report, Manubot (2019)
24. Komodo Team (2018). https://github.com/KomodoPlatform/BarterDEX
25. Ton, N.: A complete list of cryptocurrency exchange hacks [updated], July 2020. https://blog.idex.io/all-posts/a-complete-list-of-cryptocurrency-exchange-hacks-updated
26. Vitalik, B.: Chain interoperability (2016)
27. Wood, G.: Polkadot: vision for a heterogeneous multi-chain framework. https://github.com/polkadot-io/polkadotpaper/raw/master/PolkaDotPaper.pdf
28. Xu, J., Livshits, B.: The anatomy of a cryptocurrency pump-and-dump scheme. In: 28th USENIX Security Symposium (USENIX Security 2019), pp. 1609–1625 (2019)
29. Zakhary, V., Agrawal, D., El Abbadi, A.: Atomic commitment across blockchains. Proc. VLDB Endow. **13**(9) (2020)
30. Zamyatin, A., Harz, D., Lind, J., Panayiotou, P., Gervais, A., Knottenbelt, W.: XCLAIM: trustless, interoperable, cryptocurrency-backed assets. In: 2019 IEEE Symposium on Security and Privacy (SP), pp. 193–210 (2019). https://doi.org/10.1109/SP.2019.00085
31. Zamyatin, A.: Re-implementing BTC relay in solidity, January 2019. https://www.alexeizamyatin.me/reimplementing-btcrelay-in-solidity/

New Results on Test-Cost Minimization in Database Migration

Utku Umur Acikalin[1], Bugra Caskurlu[1], Piotr Wojciechowski[2](✉), and K. Subramani[2]

[1] Department of Computer Engineering, TOBB University of Economics and Technology, Ankara, Turkey
{u.acikalin,b.caskurlu}@etu.edu.tr

[2] LDCSEE, West Virginia University, Morgantown, WV, USA
{pwjociec,k.subramani}@mail.wvu.edu

Abstract. An important ubiquitous task in modern cloud systems is the migration of databases from one location to another. In practical settings, the databases are migrated in several shifts in order to meet the quality of service requirements of the end-users [18]. Once a batch of databases is migrated in a shift, the applications that depend on the databases on that shift are to be immediately tested [8]. Testing an application is a costly procedure [25] and the number of times an application is to be tested throughout the migration process varies greatly depending on the migration schedule. An interesting algorithmic challenge is to find a schedule that minimizes the total testing cost of all the applications. This problem, referred to as the capacity constrained database migration (CCDM) problem, is known to be **NP-hard** and fixed-parameter intractable for various relevant parameters [24]. In this paper, we provide new approximability and inapproximability results as well as new conditional lower bounds for the running time of any exact algorithm for the CCDM problem. Also, we adapt heuristic algorithms devised for the Hypergraph Partitioning problem to the CCDM problem and give extensive experimental results.

1 Introduction

Every new generation of mobile networks comes with increasingly more data intensive applications. With the introduction of the 5G broadband cellular network standard, numerous applications of the Internet-of-Things (IoT) paradigm, such as data-sweeping smart cities, are on the way from science fiction to reality [19]. Big data is becoming a household word due to the penetration of more and more data intensive technologies into the daily lives of society. Cloud solutions are now commonly in use to handle the unprecedented software, platform, and infrastructure needs of emerging technologies. Amazon Inc., known by many

---

This research was supported in part by the Air-Force Office of Scientific Research through Grant FA9550-19-1-0177 and in part by the Air-Force Research Laboratory, Rome through Contract FA8750-17-S-7007.

© Springer Nature Switzerland AG 2021
G. D'Angelo and O. Michail (Eds.): ALGOCLOUD 2021, LNCS 13084, pp. 38–55, 2021.
https://doi.org/10.1007/978-3-030-93043-1_3

as an online retail company, for instance, obtained 62% of its operating profits via Amazon Web Services in 2019 [4].

The ubiquity of computation and storage capabilities of cloud systems is undeniable. However, there are challenges with regard to resource allocation and data management [16]. One such challenge is scheduling the commonly performed task of migration of databases from one location to another due to a variety of reasons such as database software updates, changes to hardware, project standards, and other business factors [20]. Database migration is typically performed in *shifts*, i.e., a subset of databases is migrated in each shift, so as to satisfy the Quality-of-Service (QoS) requirements of the end-user applications [27]. This is an expensive procedure since when a database is migrated, every application that is dependent upon it must be immediately tested due to software reliability standards [8]. Notice that if an application is dependent on databases scheduled to migrate in k distinct shifts, then this application is to be tested k times throughout the migration schedule. Therefore, it is of vital importance to consider application-database dependencies in database migration scheduling. Subramani et al. [23] considered the database migration scheduling problem with the objective of minimizing the number of shifts used. That model is appropriate especially for security sensitive domains, and the associated combinatorial problems are related to some variants of the classical bin packing problem [26].

Patil et al. [18] introduced the cost-effective database migration scheduling problem and proved that the problem is **NP-hard**. They provided an integer programming formulation for the problem that can be used to find optimal solutions for small instances. Subramani et al. [24] formalized a very general framework for the database migration scheduling problem that subsumes the model in [18], and accommodates the needs of various enterprises with customized constraints. They presented **NP-hardness** results for all the models in their framework, as well as fixed-parameter intractability results for some relevant parameters. They also presented a randomized $(\frac{3}{2} + \epsilon)$-approximation algorithm for the most restricted model of the CCDM problem, where each application depends on at most two databases, the migration is to be performed in two shifts, and not only the testing costs of the applications but also the database sizes and the shift sizes are constant. We refer to this special case as the CCDM2 problem.

In this paper, we present approximability and inapproximability results as well as a new conditional lower bound for the running time of any exact algorithm for the CCDM problem. Specifically, we show that no $2^{o(n)}$-time algorithm exists for the CCDM2 problem, unless the Exponential Time Hypothesis (ETH) fails. Note that since the CCDM2 problem is the most restricted version of the CCDM problem, the $2^{o(n)}$ conditional lower bound for the running time holds for all the models of the CCDM problem. We also generalize the randomized $(\frac{3}{2} + \epsilon)$-approximation algorithm for the CCDM2 problem given in [24], for the models where the testing costs of the applications are not necessarily constant and the migration is to be scheduled in an arbitrary number of shifts. The approximation factor of our algorithm is $(\frac{2l-1}{l} + \epsilon)$, where l is the number of shifts to be used during the database migration process. We also show that **APX-hardness** of some models of the CCDM problem implies **APX-hardness** for the weighted Minimum Bisection problem [12]. We adapted heuristic algorithms devised for the Hypergraph Partitioning problem to the CCDM problem and tested their performance on small randomly generated instances for all the 8 models. The best performing algorithm finds solutions that are within 0.75% and 18.63% of the optimum in the average-case and worst-case respectively while solving 64.62% of the instances optimally.

The rest of this paper is organized as follows: Sect. 2 formally describes the capacity constrained database migration (CCDM) problem, using the framework given in [24]. The $2^{o(n)}$ conditional lower bound for the CCDM problem is given in Sect. 3. The approximability and inapproximability results are presented in Sect. 4. A detailed implementation profile of algorithms for CCDM variants is provided in Sect. 5. We conclude in Sect. 6, by summarizing our contributions and outlining avenues for future research.

2 Model and Preliminaries

In this section, we present the framework developed in [24] for the CCDM problem and the technical results presented therein. The framework subsumes several models, each of which is designed to accommodate the customized needs of various enterprises. We refer the reader to [24] for the respective motivation behind the models.

We have a set of m applications $\mathcal{A} = \{A_1, A_2, \ldots, A_m\}$ and a set of n databases $\mathcal{B} = \{B_1, B_2, \ldots, B_n\}$ such that each application calls at least one database. The call relationship is represented by the binary $m \times n$ matrix $\mathbf{D}$, i.e., $d_{ij} = 1$ if application A_i calls database B_j, and $d_{ij} = 0$ otherwise. Testing costs of the applications and the database sizes are represented by the vectors $\mathbf{c} = [c_1, c_2, \ldots, c_m]^T$ and $\mathbf{w} = [w_1, w_2, \ldots, w_n]^T$ respectively.

In the CCDM problem, $\mathcal{B}$ is to be partitioned into clusters, which we refer to as *shifts*. The databases in the same shift migrate at the same time and once a shift migrates, all the applications that call at least one database in that shift are to be immediately tested. The shift-size vector $\mathbf{l} = [l_1, l_2, \ldots, l_k]^T$ gives the upper bound on the total size of the databases that can migrate in each shift. The input to the CCDM problem is the 4-tuple $\langle \mathbf{c}, \mathbf{w}, \mathbf{D}, \mathbf{l} \rangle$.

The output of the CCDM problem is a clustering of $\mathcal{B}$ into shifts such that the total size of the databases in shift i is at most l_i. Notice that if the databases called by A_i are placed into x_i distinct shifts, then A_i is to be tested x_i times throughout the migration process for a testing cost of $x_i \cdot c_i$. The goal in the CCDM problem is to do the clustering so that the total application testing cost $\sum_{i=1}^{m} x_i \cdot c_i$ is minimized.

Each model of the CCDM problem is specified as a triple $\langle \alpha \mid \beta \mid \gamma \rangle$, where the values α, β, and γ take represent certain restrictions on the values of the input vectors $\mathbf{c}$, $\mathbf{w}$, and $\mathbf{l}$, respectively. We next present the potential values for the parameters α, β, and γ and their respective meanings.

(i) Application Testing cost (α):
  (a) Constant (const) - The testing cost of each application is the same.
  (b) Arbitrary (arb) - There is no relation between the testing costs of different applications.
(ii) Size of Databases (β):
  (a) Constant (const) - The size of each database is the same.
  (b) Arbitrary (arb) - There is no relation between the sizes of different databases.
(iii) Shift size (γ):
  (a) Constant (const) - The cumulative size of the databases that can migrate in each shift is bounded by the same constant L.
  (b) Arbitrary (arb) - The upper bounds on the cumulative size of the databases that can migrate in each shift are arbitrary.

Thus, the triple $\langle$const | arb | arb$\rangle$, for instance, refers to the CCDM problem in which the application testing costs are constant, the database sizes are arbitrary, and the shift sizes are arbitrary. Notice that the triple notation specifies 8 different models of the CCDM problem. In order to refer to both of the two models that differ by one parameter, we use $*$ as the corresponding entry of the triple. For instance, $\langle$const | arb | $*\rangle$ refers to both models in which the application testing costs are constant and the database sizes are arbitrary. Similarly, $\langle$const | $*$ | $*\rangle$ refers to all four of the models in which the application testing costs are constant. We refer to the CCDM problem under the model $\langle$const | const | const$\rangle$, when there are only two shifts and each application calls at most two databases, as the CCDM2 problem. Though the setting of the CCDM2 problem is rather restricted, most of the hardness results for the CCDM problem also hold for the CCDM2 problem as well.

The CCDM2 problem, and thus all the models of the CCDM problem, are known to be **NP-hard** [24]. Subramani et al. [24] investigated the fixed-parameter tractability of the CCDM problem for two separate parameters. They showed that $\langle *$ | arb | $*\rangle$ is fixed-parameter intractable, when the parameter is the number of applications. They also showed that $\langle *$ | $*$ | arb$\rangle$ is fixed-parameter intractable, when the parameter is the maximum number of applications that call a database.

3 New Algorithmic Bounds

In this section, we present a conditional lower bound on the running time of any exact algorithm for the CCDM problem. In particular, we show that, unless the Exponential Time Hypothesis (ETH) fails, there is no $2^{o(n)}$ time algorithm for the CCDM problem. In fact, we show that, unless the ETH fails, there is no $2^{o(n)}$ time algorithm for the CCDM2 problem. Note that this lower bound rules out a $O\left(2^{(n^{1-\epsilon})}\right)$ algorithm for any $\epsilon > 0$.

Consider a 3CNF formula Φ with m' clauses and n' variables. From Φ we construct a CCDM2 instance I such that Φ is NAE-satisfiable, if and only if the databases in I can be migrated with cost at most $(m' \cdot \binom{2 \cdot n'}{2} + m' \cdot n'^2 - 5 \cdot m' - 2 \cdot n')$. We construct I as follows:

1. Create two shifts S_1 and S_2 of size n'.
2. For each variable x_i, create the databases B_i^+ and B_i^- both of size 1. Additionally, create the applications $A_{i,1}$ through $A_{i,m-1}$. Each of these applications has cost 1 and uses the databases B_i^+ and B_i^-.
3. For each pair of variables x_i and x_j, $i < j$, and each clause ϕ_k:
   (a) If ϕ_k uses the literals x_i and x_j, then create the following applications with cost 1:
      i. The application $A_{i,j,k}^{+-}$ using the databases B_i^+ and B_j^-.
      ii. The application $A_{i,j,k}^{-+}$ using the databases B_i^- and B_j^+.
      iii. The application $A_{i,j,k}^{--}$ using the databases B_i^- and B_j^-.
   (b) If ϕ_k uses the literals x_i and $\neg x_j$, then create the following applications with cost 1:
      i. The application $A_{i,j,k}^{++}$ using the databases B_i^+ and B_j^+.
      ii. The application $A_{i,j,k}^{-+}$ using the databases B_i^- and B_j^+.
      iii. The application $A_{i,j,k}^{--}$ using the databases B_i^- and B_j^-.
   (c) If ϕ_k uses the literals $\neg x_i$ and x_j, then create the following applications with cost 1:
      i. The application $A_{i,j,k}^{++}$ using the databases B_i^+ and B_j^+.
      ii. The application $A_{i,j,k}^{+-}$ using the databases B_i^+ and B_j^-.
      iii. The application $A_{i,j,k}^{--}$ using the databases B_i^- and B_j^-.
   (d) If ϕ_k uses the literals $\neg x_i$ and $\neg x_j$, then create the following applications with cost 1:
      i. The application $A_{i,j,k}^{++}$ using the databases B_i^+ and B_j^+.
      ii. The application $A_{i,j,k}^{+-}$ using the databases B_i^+ and B_j^-.
      iii. The application $A_{i,j,k}^{-+}$ using the databases B_i^- and B_j^+.
   (e) If ϕ_k does not use both of the variables, then create the following applications with cost 1:
      i. The application $A_{i,j,k}^{++}$ using the databases B_i^+ and B_j^+.
      ii. The application $A_{i,j,k}^{+-}$ using the databases B_i^+ and B_j^-.
      iii. The application $A_{i,j,k}^{-+}$ using the databases B_i^- and B_j^+.
      iv. The application $A_{i,j,k}^{--}$ using the databases B_i^- and B_j^-.

From Φ, we also create the CCDM2 instance I' with the same shifts and databases as I, but with the following applications:

1. For each variable x_i, create the application $A_{i,m}$ with cost 1 that uses the databases B_i^+ and B_i^-.
2. For each clause $\phi_k = (l_i \vee l_j \vee l_h)$, $i < j < h$, create:
   (a) The application $A_{i,j,k}^{s_i s_j}$ using databases $B_i^{s_i}$ and $B_j^{s_j}$ where s_i and s_j are the signs of literals l_i and l_j ($s_i = +$ if l_i is a positive literal and $s_i = -$ if l_i is a negative literal).
   (b) The application $A_{i,h,k}^{s_i s_h}$ using databases $B_i^{s_i}$ and $B_h^{s_h}$.
   (c) The application $A_{j,h,k}^{s_j s_h}$ using databases $B_j^{s_j}$ and $B_h^{s_h}$.

Note that I' has $(n' + 3 \cdot m')$ applications. Additionally, note that no application in I' is in I and that, when considering both I and I', there are a total of m applications using each pair of databases. Thus, there are a total of $(m' \cdot \binom{2 \cdot n'}{2} - 3 \cdot m' - n')$ applications in I.

Lemma 1 states that Φ is NAE-satisfiable, if and only if the databases in I can be migrated with cost at most $(m' \cdot \binom{2 \cdot n'}{2} + m' \cdot n'^2 - 5 \cdot m' - 2 \cdot n')$.

Lemma 1. *Let Φ be a 3CNF formula and let I and I' be the CCDM2 instances created from Φ. Φ is NAE-satisfiable, if and only if the databases in I can be migrated with cost at most $(m' \cdot \binom{2 \cdot n'}{2} + m' \cdot n'^2 - 5 \cdot m' - 2 \cdot n')$.*

Proof. Note that migrating the databases in I has total cost at most $(m' \cdot \binom{2 \cdot n'}{2} + m' \cdot n'^2 - 5 \cdot m' - 2 \cdot n')$, if and only if at most $(m' \cdot n'^2 - 2 \cdot m' - n')$ applications in I need to be tested twice. In any database migration, a total of $m' \cdot n'^2$ applications need to be tested twice if we consider both the applications in I and the applications in I'. Thus, migrating the databases in I has total cost at most $(m' \cdot \binom{2 \cdot n'}{2} + m' \cdot n'^2 - 5 \cdot m' - 2 \cdot n')$, if and only if at least $(2 \cdot m' + n')$ applications in I' need to be tested twice.

Let M be a migration of the databases such that at least $(2 \cdot m' + n')$ applications in I' need to be tested twice. Let $\mathbf{x}$ be an assignment to the variables in Φ such that x_i is assigned **true** if database B_i^+ is assigned to shift S_1 and **false** otherwise.

Consider the clause $\phi_k = (l_i \vee l_j \vee l_h)$. Let s_i, s_j, and s_h be the signs of literals l_i, l_j, and l_h. If the databases $B_i^{s_i}$, $B_j^{s_j}$, and $B_h^{s_h}$ are all assigned to the same shift then none of the applications $A_{i,j,k}^{s_i s_j}$, $A_{i,h,k}^{s_i s_h}$, $A_{j,h,k}^{s_j s_h}$ need to be tested twice. If the databases are assigned to separate shifts, then it must be the case that two databases are assigned to one shift and one database is assigned to the other shift. Thus, two of these applications will need to be tested twice and one application will need to be tested once. Consequently, no migration will test more than $2 \cdot m'$ of the applications in I' associated with clauses of Φ twice.

Thus, M needs to test all n' applications in I' associated with the variables of Φ twice. This means that for each i, the databases B_i^+ and B_i^- are assigned to separate shifts. Thus, if x_i is assigned **true**, then $B_i^+ \in S_1$ and $B_i^- \in S_2$. Conversely, if x_i is assigned **false**, then $B_i^+ \in S_2$ and $B_i^- \in S_1$. From the arguments made previously, at least two of the applications associated with the clause ϕ_k need to be tested twice. Thus, at least one of the literals in ϕ_k is assigned **true** and at least one of the literals in ϕ_k is assigned **false**. Consequently, $\mathbf{x}$ NAE-satisfies Φ.

Now assume that $\mathbf{x}$ is an assignment that NAE-satisfies Φ. From $\mathbf{x}$ we construct a migration M of the databases in I as follows:

For each variable x_i:

1. If x_i is assigned **true** by $\mathbf{x}$, then assign B_i^+ to shift S_1 and B_i^- to shift S_2.
2. If x_i is assigned **false** by $\mathbf{x}$, then assign B_i^+ to shift S_2 and B_i^- to shift S_1.

Note that M tests all n' applications in I' associated with the variables of Φ twice.

Consider the clause $\phi_k = (l_i \vee l_j \vee l_h)$. Let s_i, s_j, and s_h be the signs of literals l_i, l_j, and l_h. Since $\mathbf{x}$ NAE-satisfies Φ, at least one literal in ϕ_k is **true** and at least one literal is **false**. If all three databases $B_i^{s_i}$, $B_j^{s_j}$, and $B_h^{s_h}$ were assigned to the same shift, then by construction of M, $\mathbf{x}$ would either set all three literals in ϕ_k to **true** or it would set all three literals in ϕ_k to **false**. Since $\mathbf{x}$ NAE-satisfies Φ, this cannot happen. Thus, the databases $B_i^{s_i}$, $B_j^{s_j}$, and $B_h^{s_h}$ need to be assigned to separate shifts. Consequently, two of the applications $A_{i,j,k}^{s_i s_j}$, $A_{i,h,k}^{s_i s_h}$, $A_{j,h,k}^{s_j s_h}$ need to be tested twice. This means that M tests $2 \cdot m'$ of the applications in I' associated with clauses of Φ twice.

A total of $(n' + 2 \cdot m')$ applications in I' need to be tested twice. From the arguments used previously, this means that migrating the databases in I has total cost at most $(m' \cdot \binom{2 \cdot n'}{2} + m' \cdot n'^2 - 5 \cdot m' - 2 \cdot n')$ as desired. □

Theorem 1 establishes the desired lower bound for the running time of any algorithm for the CCDM2 problem via application of the Sparsification Lemma [11].

Theorem 1. *Unless the ETH fails, the CCDM2 problem cannot be solved in time* $2^{o(n)}$.

Proof. Let Φ' be a 3-CNF formula with m^* clauses and n^* variables. From Φ' we can easily construct a 3-CNF formula Φ with $n' \in O(m^*)$ variables and $m' \in O(m^*)$ clauses such that Φ is NAE-satisfiable if and only if Φ' is satisfiable [21].

From Φ, we can construct a CCDM2 instance I with $n = 2 \cdot n' \in O(m^*)$ databases. From Lemma 1, Φ is NAE-satisfiable, if and only if the databases in I can be migrated with cost at most $(m' \cdot \binom{2 \cdot n'}{2} + m' \cdot n'^2 - 5 \cdot m' - 2 \cdot n')$. Thus, if an algorithm can solve the CCDM2 problem in $2^{o(n)}$ time, then 3-SAT could be solved in $2^{o(m^*)}$ time.

From the Sparsification Lemma, this violates the ETH [11]. □

4 Approximation Complexity

In this section, we first present Algorithm 4.1, which is a randomized algorithm for the CCDM problem under the models $\langle * \mid \text{const} \mid \text{const} \rangle$, with the restriction that each application calls at most two databases.

Function MIN-TEST-COST($\langle \mathbf{c}, \mathbf{w}, \mathbf{D}, \mathbf{l} \rangle$, ϵ)

1: **if** $n < 1 + \frac{l-1}{l \cdot \epsilon}$ **then**
2: Find an optimal solution using brute force.
3: **else**
4: Let $i = 1$.
5: **while** there are unassigned databases **do**
6: Select $\frac{n}{l}$ of the unassigned databases uniformly and at random.
7: Assign the selected databases to the shift i.
8: $i = i + 1$.
9: **end while**
10: **end if**

Algorithm 4.1: Approximation algorithm for the models $\langle * \mid \text{const} \mid \text{const} \rangle$ under the restriction that each application calls at most two databases.

Theorem 2 establishes the approximation factor of Algorithm 4.1 by bounding the expected number of times each application is tested in the schedule generated by Algorithm 4.1.

Theorem 2. *For any given $\epsilon > 0$, Algorithm 4.1 returns a solution whose total application testing cost is at most $(\frac{2 \cdot l - 1}{l} + \epsilon)$ times that of the optimum, for the CCDM problem under the models $\langle * \mid \text{const} \mid \text{const} \rangle$, when each application calls at most two databases.*

Proof. Since Algorithm 4.1 finds the optimal solution in polynomial time by brute force if $n < 1 + \frac{l-1}{l \cdot \epsilon}$, in the rest of the proof, we will assume the contrary, i.e., $\epsilon \geq \frac{l-1}{l \cdot (n-1)}$.

Let X_i be a random variable denoting the number of times application A_i is tested in the schedule generated by Algorithm 4.1. Notice that $X_i \in \{1, 2\}$ for all i, since each application calls at most two databases. The total application testing cost of the schedule returned by Algorithm 4.1 is $\sum_{i=1}^{m} c_i \cdot X_i$. Note that $\sum_{i=1}^{m} c_i$ is a lower bound for the cost of the optimal solution, since each application is to be tested at least once. To complete the proof, all we need to do is to show that $\mathbb{E}(\sum_{i=1}^{m} c_i \cdot X_i) \leq (\frac{2 \cdot l - 1}{l} + \epsilon) \cdot \sum_{i=1}^{m} c_i$. Due to linearity of expectations, it suffices to show that $\mathbb{E}(X_i) \leq (\frac{2 \cdot l - 1}{l} + \epsilon)$ for any i. If A_i calls exactly one database then this inequality is trivially satisfied since $\mathbb{E}(X_i) = 1$. So, in the rest of the proof, without loss of generality, we only consider applications that call exactly two databases.

Let A_i be an application that calls databases B_j and B_k. Let E_i denote the event that databases B_j and B_k are assigned to the same shift. Accordingly, $\overline{E_i}$ is the event that the databases B_j and B_k are assigned to different shifts. $\mathbb{E}(X_i)$ can be bounded as follows:

$$\begin{aligned}
\mathbb{E}(X_i) &= 1 \cdot \mathbf{Pr}(E_i) + 2 \cdot \mathbf{Pr}(\overline{E_i}) \\
&= 1 \cdot \left(\frac{\frac{n}{l}-1}{n-1}\right) + 2 \cdot \left(1 - \left(\frac{\frac{n}{l}-1}{n-1}\right)\right) = 2 - \left(\frac{\frac{n}{l}-1}{n-1}\right) \\
&= 2 - \frac{n-l}{l \cdot (n-1)} = 2 - \left(\frac{n-1}{l \cdot (n-1)} + \frac{1-l}{l \cdot (n-1)}\right) \\
&= 2 - \frac{n-1}{l \cdot (n-1)} + \frac{l-1}{l \cdot (n-1)} = 2 - \frac{1}{l} + \frac{l-1}{l \cdot (n-1)} \\
&= \frac{2 \cdot l - 1}{l} + \frac{l-1}{l \cdot (n-1)} \\
&\leq \frac{2 \cdot l - 1}{l} + \epsilon, \text{ as desired.}
\end{aligned}$$

□

The Minimum Bisection problem and its variants are among the most intriguing problems in the area of approximation algorithms [12]. This is probably because very little is known regarding their approximability. For instance, though the best approximation algorithm for the Minimum Bisection problem achieves a guarantee of $O(\log^{1.5} n)$ [15], there is no result that rules out the possibility of a PTAS. In the weighted Minimum Bisection problem, we are given an edge-weighted undirected graph $G = (V, E)$, and the goal is to partition V into V_1 and V_2 such that $||V_1| - |V_2|| \leq 1$, and the sum of the weights of the edges with endpoints in different sets is as small as possible. Theorem 3 below establishes that **APX-hardness** of some variant of the CCDM problem implies the same for the weighted Minimum Bisection problem.

Theorem 3. *If the CCDM problem under the models* $\langle * \mid \text{const} \mid \text{const} \rangle$*, with the restrictions that there are two shifts and each application calls at most two databases, is* **APX-hard***, then the weighted Minimum Bisection problem is* **APX-hard**.

Proof. Assume that the CCDM problem, under the models $\langle * \mid \text{const} \mid \text{const} \rangle$ with the restrictions that there are two shifts and each application calls at most two databases, is **APX-hard**. All we need is to prove that the weighted Minimum Bisection problem is **APX-hard** under this assumption. We will do that via a PTAS reduction to the weighted Minimum Bisection problem [17].

Given a CCDM instance $\mathcal{I}$ satisfying the aforementioned restrictions, we construct a corresponding weighted Minimum Bisection instance $\mathcal{F}$ as follows:

1. For each database B_i of $\mathcal{I}$, create a vertex v_i in $\mathcal{F}$, i.e., the vertex set of $\mathcal{F}$ is $V = \{v_1, \cdots, v_n\}$.
2. For each application A_i of $\mathcal{I}$ that calls exactly two databases, say B_j and B_k, create the (v_j, v_k) edge in $\mathcal{F}$ with weight c_i.
3. If there are multiple edges between a pair of vertices in $\mathcal{F}$, replace them with a single edge whose weight is the sum of the weights of the replaced edges.

Given $\mathcal{I}$, one can construct $\mathcal{F}$ in polynomial-time as described above and the size of $\mathcal{F}$ is no more than the size of $\mathcal{I}$. Thus this construction forms the function f required for a PTAS reduction.

Let o and o' denote the value of the optimal solutions for the instances $\mathcal{F}$ and $\mathcal{I}$, respectively. Let C_T represent the total testing of all applications once in $\mathcal{I}$, i.e., $C_T = \sum_{A_i \in \mathcal{I}} c_i$. Notice that $o' = o + C_T$. Without loss of generality, assume that $o > 0$. This is because it is trivial to decide whether the optimal solution to a weighted Minimum Bisection problem is 0 or not.

For any $\epsilon > 0$, let a be an $(1+\epsilon)$-approximate solution for the weighted Minimum Bisection problem. We construct the solution a' for $\mathcal{I}$ using a as follows. For each vertex $v_i \in \mathcal{F}$, if $v_i \in V_1$ in a then assign the corresponding database B_i to the first shift in a'. Otherwise, assign B_i to the second shift in a'. This forms the function g required for a PTAS reduction.

Let z and z' denote the objective function values of a and a', respectively. Let $\alpha(\epsilon) = \epsilon$ be the last function required for a PTAS reduction. All we need to show is $\frac{z'}{o'} \leq 1 + \alpha(\epsilon) = (1+\epsilon)$. To do this we use the facts that $z' = z + C_T$ and $o' = o + C_T$. Thus,

$$\frac{z'}{o'} = \frac{z + C_T}{o + C_T} \leq \frac{z}{o} \leq 1 + \epsilon$$

holds since $C_T > 0$ and $z \geq o$.

This means that the reduction from the CCDM problem to the weighted Minimum Bisection problem is a PTAS reduction. Thus, if the CCDM problem is **APX-hard**, so is the weighted Minimum Bisection problem. □

5 Empirical Analysis

Each model of the CCDM problem is related to a variant of the Hypergraph Partitioning (HGP) problem [13]. The heuristic algorithms for the HGP problem, except PaToH [3] and KaHyPar [1], are not particularly useful for the models of the CCDM problem with arbitrary shift sizes. Thus, we base our experimental analysis on PaToH and KaHyPar. In Sect. 5.1, we present the HPG problem as well as the PaToH and KaHyPar algorithms. In Sect. 5.2, we describe our instance generation procedure and the experimental setup. In Sect. 5.3, we tabulate the performance of the adaptations of PaToH and KaHyPar on a rich set of randomly generated CCDM instances.

5.1 The Hypergraph Partitioning Problem and Heuristics

An undirected hypergraph H is a binary pair (V, N), where V is a set of vertices with weights $w : V \rightarrow \mathcal{R}_{\geq 0}$, and N is a set of nets (hyperedges) with weights $c : N \rightarrow \mathcal{R}_{\geq 0}$. A k-way partition $\Pi = \{V_1, V_2, \ldots, V_k\}$ of V into k blocks is called *balanced* if each block satisfies the balance constraint $\sum_{v \in V_i} w(v) \leq (1+\epsilon) \cdot W_{avg}$ where $W_{avg} = \frac{\sum_{v \in V} w(v)}{|V|}$, and ϵ is called maximum imbalance ratio.

Given a hypergraph $H = (V, N)$, a number of blocks k, and a maximum imbalance ratio ϵ, *k-way Hypergraph Partitioning* problem is to find a balanced k-way partition Π that minimizes an objective function defined over the nets. The Sum of External Degree (SOED) objective function is the most similar to the objective function in the CCDM problem and is defined as $soed(\pi) = \sum_{e \in N} c(e) \cdot \lambda(e)$, where $\lambda(e)$ denotes the number of blocks that contains a vertex of e.

The models of the CCDM problem with constant shift sizes are similar to the variants of the k-way HGP problem, whereas the models with arbitrary shift sizes are similar to a more general hypergraph partitioning setting with variable block sizes. The main difference between the CCDM problem and the HGP problem variants is that in the CCDM problem, not all shifts need to be used, whereas in the k-way HGP problem, each block is necessarily non-empty.

Since the k-way HGP problem is **NP-hard** [6], a large amount of effort is put into heuristic algorithms [1–3,10,13,14,22] to tackle the problem in practice. Most of these heuristic algorithms use the *multilevel* hypergraph partitioning scheme, which consists of the following three stages: *coarsening*, *initial partitioning*, *uncoarsening*. In the coarsening stage, vertices or nets of the hypergraph are contracted to obtain series of smaller hypergraphs. In the initial partitioning stage, an initial partition is obtained by partitioning the smallest hypergraph either by computing k-way partition directly or using recursive bisectioning until k blocks are found. In the uncoarsening stage, the initial partition is uncoarsened back to obtain solutions to the larger hypergraphs until a solution to the original hypergraph is obtained. A local search procedure is used at each level of the uncoarsening stage for a more global view. The most commonly used local search procedure is the FM [5] heuristic.

PaToH uses a multilevel hypergraph partitioning scheme and recursive bisectioning to find an initial partition and a variation of the FM heuristic in the uncoarsening stages. It provides three different settings: speed, default, and quality. We use it on both default and quality settings with their default parameters. We refer to them as PaToH-D and PaToH-Q, respectively.

KaHyPar is an n-level hypergraph partitioning framework developed from a series of papers [1,2,7,9,10,22]. The latest version of the direct k-way partitioner in KaHyPar, which is referred to as KaHyPar-K, uses an n-level hypergraph partitioning scheme. As the local search algorithm, it uses an FM-based heuristic along with the Minimum Flow Refinement heuristic (MFR) [7]. There is also a meta-heuristic in KaHyPar, which is referred to as KaHyPar-E, that employs a sophisticated genetic algorithm that uses recombination and mutation operators specifically tailored for the HGP problem to explore the solution space efficiently (for more details, see [2]).

While KaHyPar-K and KaHyPar-E support variable block sizes, PaToH-D and PaToH-Q can take *target* block sizes. Target block sizes do not correspond to the maximum block size; rather, they are the desired sizes of the blocks. All heuristics use all the k blocks necessarily since they find k-way partitions. However, in the CCDM problem, not all shifts need to be used. Furthermore, our initial experiments showed that PaToH-D and PaToH-Q might compromise solution quality to respect the target block sizes. Therefore, we made the following adaptations to the heuristic algorithms.

Adaptations: We first sort the blocks in the decreasing order of their sizes. Let $L_i = \sum_{j=1}^{i} l_i$, where l_i denotes size of the block i, and let $W_t = \sum_{v \in V} w(v)$. Let x be the smallest integer such that $L_x \geq W_t$. In our experiments, we run KaHyPar-E multiple times with different numbers of blocks ranging between x and k. In order to prevent PaToH-D and PaToH-Q from compromising solution quality to respect the target block sizes, we run them multiple times with different numbers of blocks. For each number of blocks i such that $L_i \geq W_t$, we first run PaToH-D and PaToH-Q with the first i blocks having their original block sizes as their target block sizes. We then decrease the size of the last block by one and run it again until either the new total block size is less than the total vertex size, or the last block size is less than 0 to obtain more diverse partitions. To make a fair comparison between PaToH-D, PaToH-Q, and KaHyPar-K, we run KaHyPar-K the same number of times for each number of blocks but without changing the last block size.

5.2 Instance Generation and Experimental Setup

The parameters that are the same for all the 8 models are described below.

- Number of databases (n): We select 3 values for n: $10, 15, 20$.
- Number of applications (m): We select 3 values for m: $2 \cdot n, 3 \cdot n, 5 \cdot n$.
- Number of shifts (k): We select 4 values for k: $2, 3, 4, 5$.
- Number of databases called by applications (p): For each application, p is chosen uniformly and at random from $\{2, 3, 4, 5\}$ and then p databases are selected uniformly and at random.

For each of these parameters, we generate 10 instances, which adds up to $360 (= 3 \cdot 3 \cdot 4 \cdot 10)$ instances. We ensure that each database is called by at least one application. Database sizes and application testing costs in these instances are chosen according to their respective models. For models with arbitrary database sizes or application testing costs, they are chosen uniformly and at random from $\{1, \ldots, 10\}$, and they are chosen as 1 for the models with constant database sizes or constant application testing costs. 3 shift sizes with different levels of imbalance are chosen for all the generated instances to extend them into a total of 1080 instances for each model, and 8640 instances in total.

For the models with constant shift sizes and constant database sizes, we choose shift sizes as $(\lceil W_{avg} \rceil + \epsilon)$, $\forall \epsilon = 0, 1, 2$. For the models with constant shift sizes and arbitrary database sizes, we choose shift sizes as $\lceil (1 + \epsilon) \cdot W_{avg} \rceil$, $\forall \epsilon = 0.1, 0.2, 0.3$.

For the models with arbitrary shift sizes and constant database sizes, for shift k, $l_k = \lceil W_{avg} \rceil + \epsilon_k$, where ϵ_k is chosen uniformly and at random from $\{0, 1, 2\}$, $\{0, \ldots, 4\}$, $\{0, \ldots, 6\}$. For the models with arbitrary shift sizes and arbitrary database sizes, for shift i, $l_i = \lceil (1 + \epsilon_i) \cdot W_{avg} \rceil$, where ϵ_i is chosen uniformly and at random from [0, 0.2], [0, 0.4], [0, 0.6]. Optimal solutions for these instances are found by solving the following Integer Linear Program (ILP):

$$
\begin{array}{lll}
\text{minimize} \displaystyle\sum_{i=1}^{m} c_i x_i & & \\
\text{subject to} & & \\
\displaystyle\sum_{k=1}^{n} b_{jk} & = 1, & \forall j = 1,\ldots,n \\
\displaystyle\sum_{j=1}^{n} w_j \cdot b_{jk} & \leq l_k, & \forall k = 1,\ldots,n \\
\displaystyle\sum_{j=1}^{n} b_{jk} d_{ik} & \leq M_i a_{ik}, & \forall i = 1,\ldots,m, \forall k = 1,\ldots,n, \\
\displaystyle\sum_{k=1}^{n} a_{ik} & = x_i, & \forall i = 1,\ldots,m \\
b_{jk} \in \{0,1\}, & & \forall j,k = 1,\ldots,n \\
a_{ik} \in \{0,1\}, & & \forall i = 1,\ldots,m, \forall k = 1,\ldots,n \\
x_i \in \{1,\ldots,n\}, & & \forall i = 1,\ldots,m
\end{array}
\tag{1}
$$

In System (1), decision variable b_{jk} equals 1 if the database B_j is assigned to shift k and 0 otherwise. Decision variable a_{ik} equals 1 if the application A_i needs to be tested after the shift k is migrated, 0 otherwise. Decision variable x_i equals the number of times the application A_i needs to be tested after all migrations.

The first set of constraints ensures that each database is assigned to a shift. The second set of constraints enforces the shift sizes. The parameter M_i is equal to the number of databases used by application A_i, i.e., $M_i = \sum_{j=1}^{n} d_{ij}$. The third set of constraints sets a_{ik} to 1 if any of the databases used by the application A_i is assigned to the shift k. The last set of constraints counts how many times the application A_i needs to be tested after all shifts are migrated.

Experimental Setup. All experiments are performed on the same computer that has a 64-bit AMD Ryzen 7 2700X CPU and 32 GB DDR4 3200 MHz RAM running Ubuntu 18.04.02. The ILP given in System (1) is implemented in Java version 8 and solved using CPLEX version 12.6.2. The ILP uses all 8 cores with 16 threads while the heuristic algorithms use a single core.

5.3 Performance of the Heuristic Algorithms

Recall that we generated a total of 8640 instances of the CCDM problem. On each of these instances, we ran CPLEX on the ILP given in System (1) to generate an optimal solution. For each heuristic, we used the relative gap between the solution generated by the heuristic and the optimal solution generated by CPLEX to measure the quality of that heuristic.

Several of the 8640 total instances were discarded for a variety of reasons. Three instances were discarded because CPLEX declared them to be infeasible. An additional 8 instances were discarded because CPLEX was unable to solve them due to lack of memory. Finally, 413 instances were discarded because at least one of the heuristics was unable to find a feasible solution. Table 1 details the distribution of these discarded instances.

Table 1. Table shows the number of infeasible instances, average and maximum relative gaps from the optimal solution for each algorithm

Model	PaToH-D			PaToH-Q			KaHyPar-K			KaHyPar-E		
	Inf	Avg	Max	Inf	Avg	Max	Inf	Avg	Max	Inf	Avg	Max
⟨arb | arb | const⟩	50	2.89	16.77	69	2.38	18.15	20	1.10	12.07	20	0.55	12.07
⟨const | arb | const⟩	47	2.52	18.18	61	2.13	14.05	10	1.01	10.53	12	0.45	7.69
⟨arb | const | const⟩	0	1.53	11.50	0	1.21	11.50	0	0.77	6.91	0	0.47	6.47
⟨const | const | const⟩	0	1.35	10.29	0	1.10	8.33	0	0.77	6.90	0	0.40	4.76
⟨arb | arb | arb⟩	41	3.62	20.28	58	2.97	20.28	8	2.35	16.83	11	1.40	14.93
⟨const | arb | arb⟩	31	3.18	17.91	44	2.75	18.64	6	2.27	16.92	3	1.39	16.00
⟨arb | const | arb⟩	0	1.78	15.84	0	1.41	22.98	0	1.50	25.00	0	0.71	18.63
⟨const | const | arb⟩	0	1.61	12.68	0	1.28	12.68	0	1.46	22.00	0	0.64	7.58
Total	169	2.28	20.28	232	1.87	22.98	44	1.40	25.00	46	0.75	18.63

As seen in Table 1, the heuristic algorithms perform better on CCDM instances in which database size is constant than they do on instances in which database size is arbitrary. Additionally, the heuristics perform better on instances with a constant application testing cost than they do on instances with arbitrary application testing costs. However, the improvement in performance is smaller than the improvement seen between arbitrary and constant database size.

On average, PaToH-Q returns solutions closer to the optimum solution than PaToH-D. However, PaToH-Q failed to find a feasible solution on more instances than PaToH-D did. KaHyPar-K and KaHyPar-E could not find feasible solutions for 44 and 46 instances, respectively.

Figure 1 shows that KaHyPar-E outperforms all other algorithms and solves 64.62% of the instances optimally. KaHyPar-K, PaToH-Q, and PaToH-D solve 51.20%, 44.11%, 34.02% of the instances optimally, respectively. KaHyPar-E, KaHyPar-K, PaToH-Q, and PaToH-D find solutions that are 2.58%, 4.22%, 5.29%, 5.88% within the optimal in 90% of the instances.

Table 2 shows that KaHyPar-K finds solutions that are closer to optimal than the solutions found by PaToH-D and PaToH-Q in 3673 and 2509 instances respectively. However, PaToH-D and PaToH-Q find solutions that are closer to optimal in 1240 and 1421 instances respectively. There are only on 3 instances in which KaHyPar-K finds a solution closer to optimal than the solution found by KaHyPar-E. Interestingly, PaToH-D and PaToH-Q find better solutions on 500 and 515 instances respectively, when compared to KaHyPar-E.

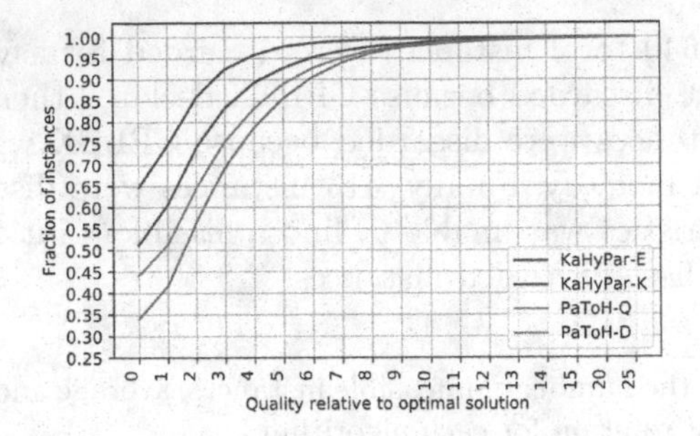

Fig. 1. Relative gap of all algorithms with respect to the fraction of the instances

Table 2. Each row of the table corresponds to the percentage of instances that algorithm find better solutions compared to the other algorithm

Algorithm				
Algorithm	PaToH-D	PaToH-Q	KaHyPar-K	KaHyPar-E
PaToH-D	–	10.81	15.09	6.09
PaToH-Q	30.55	–	17.30	6.27
KaHyPar-K	44.71	30.54	–	0.04
KaHyPar-E	54.60	41.82	27.48	–

Table 3 shows that for the instances with arbitrary database sizes, we execute the heuristic algorithms 2.5 to 3 times more when compared to the instances with constant database sizes. This has a noticeable effect on the average running times. Since we run PaToH-D, PaToH-Q, and KaHyPar-K the same number of times, we can compare their running times directly. PaToH-D is approximately 11 times faster than PaToH-Q and 95 times faster than KaHyPar-K on average. The average running time of CPLEX on the ILP is 42.7 s, whereas the maximum running time is slightly over 4.5 h.

Table 3. Table shows the average and maximum running times in milliseconds and the number of times the heuristic algorithms executed

Model	Avg. run	Algorithm							
		PaToH-D		PaToH-Q		KaHyPar-K		ILP	
		Avg.	Max	Avg.	Max	Avg.	Max	Avg.	Max
⟨arb | arb | const⟩	21.87	3.28	16	35.58	178	289.12	1420	12411.29	1782507
⟨const | arb | const⟩	21.70	3.15	16	33.63	165	289.01	1334	12023.01	1792407
⟨arb | const | const⟩	7.44	0.97	6	10.79	56	98.62	549	19678.54	2961430
⟨const | const | const⟩	7.44	0.95	5	10.66	56	99.07	548	25947.16	2667573
⟨arb | arb | arb⟩	22.25	3.30	22	35.75	225	299.95	1930	81353.22	16471270
⟨const | arb | arb⟩	22.06	3.20	20	33.46	214	298.04	1879	99503.26	16028530
⟨arb | const | arb⟩	8.93	1.15	10	12.48	109	119.96	966	33613.89	12883640
⟨const | const | arb⟩	8.93	1.14	9	12.15	104	119.81	981	53822.66	13858780
Total	14.73	2.08	22.00	22.46	225.00	197.04	1930.00	42712.74	16471270

6 Conclusion

We revisited the CCDM problem from both theoretical and experimental perspectives. On the theoretical front, we presented a new conditional lower bound for the running time of any exact algorithm as well as new approximation and inapproximability results. Specifically, we showed that there is no $2^{o(n)}$ time algorithm for any model of the CCDM problem unless the ETH fails. Moreover, we provided a randomized $(\frac{2 \cdot l-1}{l} + \epsilon)$-approximation algorithm for the CCDM problem under the models $\langle * \mid \text{const} \mid \text{const} \rangle$, when each application calls at most two databases. We finally showed that **APX-hardness** of the CCDM problem under the models $\langle * \mid \text{const} \mid \text{const} \rangle$, with the restrictions that there are two shifts and each application calls at most two databases, implies **APX-hardness** of the weighted Minimum Bisection problem.

On the experimental front, we tested the performance of the adaptations of the well-known heuristics PaToH-D, PaToH-Q, and KaHyPar-K and the well-known meta-heuristic KaHyPar-E developed for the HGP problem on randomly generated instances of each model of the CCDM problem. Our results indicate that KaHyPar-E outperforms the other heuristics. KaHyPar-E found solutions that are 0.75% within optimal on average, and it solved 64.62% of the instances optimally.

From our perspective, the following avenues of research on the theoretical front are interesting:

1. Derandomizing the randomized $(\frac{2 \cdot l-1}{l} + \epsilon)$-approximation algorithm.
2. Designing approximation algorithms and inapproximability results for all the models of the CCDM problem.

References

1. Akhremtsev, Y., Heuer, T., Sanders, P., Schlag, S.: Engineering a direct k-way hypergraph partitioning algorithm. In: 19th Workshop on Algorithm Engineering and Experiments (ALENEX 2017), pp. 28–42 (2017)
2. Andre, R., Schlag, S., Schulz, C.: Memetic multilevel hypergraph partitioning. In: Proceedings of the Genetic and Evolutionary Computation Conference, pp. 347–354 (2018)
3. Catalyurek, U.V., Aykanat, C.: Hypergraph-partitioning-based decomposition for parallel sparse-matrix vector multiplication. IEEE Trans. Parallel Distrib. Syst. **10**(7), 673–693 (1999)
4. Cohan, P.: How much of Amazon's $7.3 billion AWS profit will rivals win? (2020)
5. Fiduccia, C.M., Mattheyses, R.M.: A linear-time heuristic for improving network partitions. In: 19th Design Automation Conference, pp. 175–181. IEEE (1982)
6. Garey, M.R., Johnson, D.S.: Computers and Intractability: A Guide to the Theory of NP-Completeness. W. H. Freeman, New York (1979)
7. Gottesbüren, L., Hamann, M., Schlag, S., Wagner, D.: Advanced flow-based multilevel hypergraph partitioning. In: 18th International Symposium on Experimental Algorithms (SEA 2020). Schloss Dagstuhl-Leibniz-Zentrum für Informatik (2020)

8. Harrold, M.J., et al.: Regression test selection for Java software. ACM Sigplan Not. **36**(11), 312–326 (2001)
9. Heuer, T., Sanders, P., Schlag, S.: Network flow-based refinement for multilevel hypergraph partitioning. J. Exp. Algorithmics (JEA) **24**, 1–36 (2019)
10. Heuer, T., Schlag, S.: Improving coarsening schemes for hypergraph partitioning by exploiting community structure. In: 16th International Symposium on Experimental Algorithms (SEA 2017). Schloss Dagstuhl-Leibniz-Zentrum fuer Informatik (2017)
11. Impagliazzo, R., Paturi, R., Zane, F.: Which problems have strongly exponential complexity? J. Comput. Syst. Sci. **63**(4), 512–530 (2001)
12. Karpinski, M.: Approximability of the minimum bisection problem: an algorithmic challenge. In: Diks, K., Rytter, W. (eds.) MFCS 2002. LNCS, vol. 2420, pp. 59–67. Springer, Heidelberg (2002). https://doi.org/10.1007/3-540-45687-2_4
13. Karypis, G., Aggarwal, R., Kumar, V., Shekhar, S.: Multilevel hypergraph partitioning: applications in VLSI domain. IEEE Trans. Very Large Scale Integr. Syst. (VLSI) **7**(1), 69–79 (1999)
14. Karypis, G., Kumar, V.: Multilevel k-way hypergraph partitioning. VLSI Des. **11**(3), 285–300 (2000)
15. Krauthgamer, R., Feige, U.: A polylogarithmic approximation of the minimum bisection. SIAM Rev. **48**(1), 99–130 (2006)
16. Nascimento, D.C., Pires, C.E., Mestre, D.: Data quality monitoring of cloud databases based on data quality SLAs. In: Trovati, M., Hill, R., Anjum, A., Zhu, S.Y., Liu, L. (eds.) Big-Data Analytics and Cloud Computing, pp. 3–20. Springer, Cham (2015). https://doi.org/10.1007/978-3-319-25313-8_1
17. Orponen, P., Mannila, H.: On approximation preserving reductions: complete problems and robust measures. Technical report, Department of Computer Science, University of Helsinki (1987)
18. Patil, S., et al.: Minimizing testing overheads in database migration lifecycle. In: COMAD, p. 191 (2010)
19. Rao, S.K., Prasad, R.: Impact of 5G technologies on smart city implementation. Wirel. Pers. Communi. **100**(1), 161–176 (2018). https://doi.org/10.1007/s11277-018-5618-4
20. Ravikumar, Y.V., Krishnakumar, K.M., Basha, N.: Oracle database migration. In: Oracle Database Upgrade and Migration Methods, pp. 213–277. Springer, Berkeley (2017). https://doi.org/10.1007/978-1-4842-2328-4_5
21. Schaefer, T.J.: The complexity of satisfiability problems. In: Aho, A. (ed.) Proceedings of the 10th Annual ACM Symposium on Theory of Computing, pp. 216–226. ACM Press, New York (1978)
22. Schlag, S., Henne, V., Heuer, T., Meyerhenke, H., Sanders, P., Schulz, C.: *k*-way hypergraph partitioning via *n*-level recursive bisection. In: 18th Workshop on Algorithm Engineering and Experiments (ALENEX 2016), pp. 53–67 (2016)
23. Subramani, K., Caskurlu, B., Acikalin, U.U.: Security-aware database migration planning. In: Brandic, I., Genez, T.A.L., Pietri, I., Sakellariou, R. (eds.) ALGOCLOUD 2019. LNCS, vol. 12041, pp. 103–121. Springer, Cham (2020). https://doi.org/10.1007/978-3-030-58628-7_7
24. Subramani, K., Caskurlu, B., Velasquez, A.: Minimization of testing costs in capacity-constrained database migration. In: Disser, Y., Verykios, V.S. (eds.) ALGOCLOUD 2018. LNCS, vol. 11409, pp. 1–12. Springer, Cham (2019). https://doi.org/10.1007/978-3-030-19759-9_1
25. Vergilio, S.R., Maldonado, J.C., Jino, M., Soares, I.W.: Constraint based structural testing criteria. J. Syst. Soft. **79**(6), 756–771 (2006)

26. Wojciechowski, P., Subramani, K., Velasquez, A., Caskurlu, B.: Algorithmic analysis of priority-based bin packing. In: Mudgal, A., Subramanian, C.R. (eds.) CALDAM 2021. LNCS, vol. 12601, pp. 359–372. Springer, Cham (2021). https://doi.org/10.1007/978-3-030-67899-9_29
27. Xiaonian, W., Deng, M., Zhang, R., Zeng, B., Zhou, S.: A task scheduling algorithm based on QoS-driven in cloud computing. Procedia Comput. Sci. **17**, 1162–1169 (2013)

Privately Querying Privacy: Privacy Estimation with Guaranteed Privacy of User and Database Party

Anna Katharina Hildebrandt[1], Ernst Althaus[2(✉)], and Andreas Hildebrandt[2(✉)]

[1] MONDATA GmbH, Saarbrücken, Germany
anna.hildebrandt@mondata.de
[2] Johannes-Gutenberg University Mainz, Mainz, Germany
{ernst.althaus,andreas.hildebrandt}@uni-mainz.de

Abstract. Many fields of science and industry increasingly rely on the availability of individualized data that a given user may or may not be willing to share. Anonymization methods are often employed to improve user acceptance or are even required by law. However, the user has to rely on the technical competence and faithfulness of the database provider in implementing such measures, and even for honest and competent providers, sophisticated attacks on anonymity may still work. Consequently, many measures have been developed to allow users to estimate their anonymity in a given dataset; however, these measures are typically applied after a user has already offered his data to the provider. Here, we demonstrate how protocols based on cryptographic techniques such as secure multiparty computation and oblivious transfer can be employed to allow a user to query anonymization measures before revealing his own data without compromising the database privacy along the way.

1 Introduction

Owing to an increasing popularity of web-based services, such as social networks, and mobile devices connected to the internet, huge amounts of personal data – often of a private or sensitive nature – have today been accumulated in various data bases. Leakage of this data can have severe consequences for the individual, but occurs surprisingly often through malicious attacks or inadvertent misconfigurations. Even if the data is not exposed to third-parties, a user might have a reasonable interest in evaluating the information made available to a service provider and to restrict or even revoke it.

Privacy has been recognized as a human right as early as 1948 [7] as article 12 of the Universal Declaration of Human Rights. Today, more than 150 national constitutions state an explicit right to privacy (at the time of writing, 174 constitutions in force according to a query at https://www.constituteproject.org). Recent developments, such as the General Data Protection Regulation (GDPR) by the European Union aim at establishing the individual's control over his or her own data and thus requires to allow the user to make an informed decision about the data usage.

© Springer Nature Switzerland AG 2021
G. D'Angelo and O. Michail (Eds.): ALGOCLOUD 2021, LNCS 13084, pp. 56–72, 2021.
https://doi.org/10.1007/978-3-030-93043-1_4

Enabling such an informed decision in practice is, in our opinion, a largely unsolved problem. It is often almost or entirely impossible to truly understand the impact of data exposure due to interactions with programs or websites on privacy and anonymity. Even if such an interaction does not transmit certain highly personalized data, such as names, addresses, or social security ids, the information contained might allow a cross-correlation with other available data sets.

A famous example of such a deanonymization was demonstrated in 2008 by Narayanan and Shmatikov [22], who showed that anonymous user data made available for the so-called Netflix Challenge is so sparse that it can be successfully cross-correlated with publicly available movie ratings on the IMDB-website. This allows to match – at least in principle – IMDB user names to some of the supposedly anonymous entries from the Netflix challenge, and exposes data that a user believed to be private (his movie ratings on the anonymous Netflix system) to the public.

The sparsity of datasets which makes such correlation possible is common to many application scenarios. To give a striking example, a study by Latanya Sweeney on data from the 1990 census in the United States showed that 87% of the US population could be identified uniquely based on the combination of gender, zip code, and date of birth [24]. The situation becomes even worse in the case of medical or biological data, where it was shown, for instance, that patterns of genetic markers such as short tandem repeats allow for surname inference within the 1000 Genomes Project [12].

Consequently, considerable effort has been devoted to research on the measurement of privacy in recent years. As a result, more than 80 privacy metrics have been described in the literature, as discussed in a recent review by Wagner and Eckhoff [26]. By evaluating such metrics on his own data, a user could quantify the impact on his privacy due to data exposure to a service provider, and hence make an informed decision on whether to allow or reject data transmission. However, this approach still has a catch: a naive approach to implementing a privacy metric will require that one party has access to the data base of the service provider (or certain statistics of it, depending on the privacy metric that is to be evaluated) as well as the data of the end user.

Besides the question of practicality, a service provider will in general be unwilling to share information about his data set with the end user. The end user, on the other hand, is unwilling to share his information with the service provider before he has convinced himself – through application of the privacy metric – that his privacy will not be adversely affected. And it is hard to imagine a third-party that is trusted strongly enough by both parties that they would willingly share their information with it for the purpose of privacy metric evaluation.

1.1 Related Work

Owing to the fundamental importance of privacy, a large body of research has been devoted to its quantification [26]. To the best of our knowledge, the literature does not, however, discuss how to measure privacy *privately*, i.e., without requiring either of the parties to disclose information they would prefer to remain private. Hence, even if a service offers means by which a user can estimate his privacy with respect to this service's data set, a user is typically required to share his information with the service provider *before* he can estimate his privacy, and thus before he can make an informed decision. Should he decide that the implications for his privacy are too strong, he will need to trust the service provider to delete his data which was shared for the purpose of privacy estimation.

Alternative approaches to privacy in the online world often rely on restricting which information can be *extracted* from a database, often by using differential privacy measures. Modern implementations of these concepts allow, for instance, to perform a wide class of statistical queries with strong bounds on the privacy impact of the replies. These approaches, however, also require that the user's data is shared with the service provider and entered into the database. Only subsequent queries are protected.

1.2 Our Contribution

In this work, we address the problem of privacy estimation that respects the privacy desiderations of both, end user and database provider. To illustrate the problem statement behind our approach, consider that user Alice is interested in using Bob's cloud-based service offering. To make use of Bob's service, Alice has to share certain personal data which will be stored in Bob's internal database. Alice is concerned how this exchange of data for service will impact her own privacy (c.f. Fig. 1). Even though Alice might trust that Bob will use her data responsibly, she might not be certain that her data is safe against a potential attacker (Eve in the diagram) or that all collaborators (Charles in the diagram) of Bob are similarly trustworthy.

To assess the privacy impact of potential data misuse or leakage, Bob might offer Alice to evaluate one or several of the established privacy metrics before integrating her data into his database. Knowing the value x of a privacy metric, Alice can then use a simple thresholding ($x \geq t$?) to decide whether her privacy level is sufficient. The computation of x, however, requires input from both, Alice and Bob, to assess Alice's data in the background of Bob's existing database. Since Bob will typically be unwilling to share internal information about his database, this forces to Alice to send her data to Bob for evaluation *before* she can reasonably assess whether she is comfortable with her privacy level, and has to trust Bob not to store her data irrespective of her later decision.

In this work, we propose a solution to the problem of privately evaluating privacy metrics in the form of the PQP-protocol (Privately Querying Privacy). PQP uses a secure multiparty computation between Alice and Bob that does not require a trusted third party, but guarantees both Alice's and Bob's privacy concerns. In summary, PQP allows Alice and Bob to collaboratively evaluate certain privacy metrics (those that are based on histograms of Bob's database) without revealing information about Alice's data to Bob or vice versa.

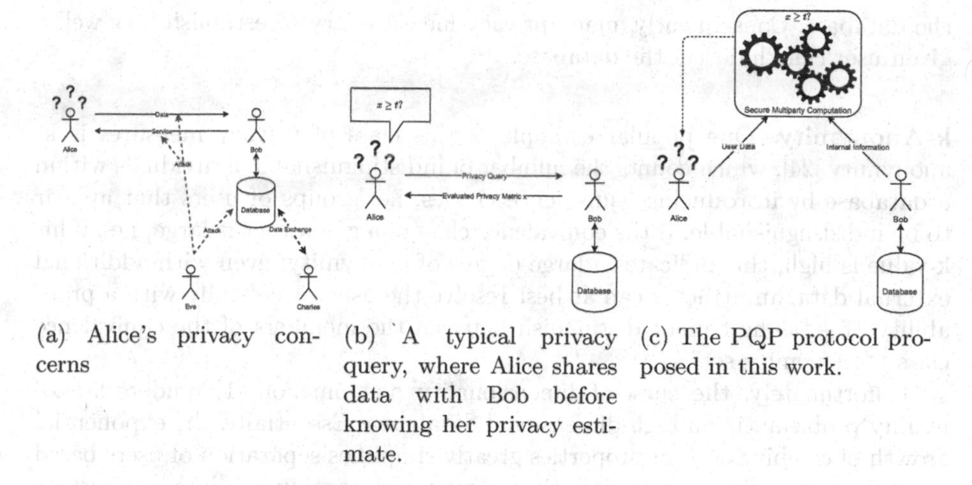

(a) Alice's privacy concerns (b) A typical privacy query, where Alice shares data with Bob before knowing her privacy estimate. (c) The PQP protocol proposed in this work.

Fig. 1. Schematic description of possible privacy concerns.

The basis of our approach are several cryptographic primitives: secure multiparty computation [27], oblivious transfer [10,23], and private set intersection [5,11].

The threat model behind our approach is that of the 'honest but curious' participant, i.e., we assume both service provider and end user to faithfully participate in the protocol, but that, given the chance, both would attempt to access private information of the other.

We demonstrate our approach on simplified models for privacy that can be used as a proxy for more sophisticated norms, summarized in the appendix.

2 Measuring Privacy and Anonymity

Scientific efforts have produced numerous privacy measures for a set of applications as diverse as social network analysis, data from car trips, or genomic samples. For a recent extensive survey on privacy metrics, see [26].

Naively, privacy is often expected to be preserved if a user's full name and address is not contained in a dataset. This view, however, is far too simplistic. Obviously, the absence of clear identifiers such as the full name is a necessary prerequisite for assuring privacy, but it is far from sufficient. In addition to the information the user wants to hide we also need to consider whether the remainder of his record in a given database will allow to infer the hidden information, either directly or through correlation with external data sources. This question cannot, typically, be answered by merely considering the type of information encoded. While the inclusion of, say, the full name will nearly always be problematic from the perspective of privacy, information about, e.g., the height or handedness of a given user might or might not be privacy-preserving, depending on the remaining properties of the record and the distribution of data in the database. Consequently, many privacy measures try to establish how well a given user can "hide" in the database.

k-Anonymity. One popular example of this class of privacy measures is k-anonymity [24], which counts the number of indistinguishable individuals within a database by introducing equivalence classes, i.e. groups of users that appear to be indistinguishable. If the equivalence class of a given user is large, i.e., if his k-value is high, this indicates a large degree of anonymity: even with additional external data, an attacker can at best resolve the user successfully with a probability of $\frac{1}{k}$, as he cannot distinguish between the members of the equivalence class ("anonymity set").

Unfortunately, the curse-of-dimensionality phenomenon [1] renders k-anonymity problematic on high-dimensional databases. Essentially, the exponential growth of combinations of properties greatly simplifies separation of users based on their properties. In practice, timestamps and continuous data are further causes for data separability.

In addition, several attacks on k-anonymity have been developed, such as homogeneity or background-knowledge attacks. Modifications of k-anonymity, such as l-diversity [20] or t-closeness [17], attempt to prevent these attack vectors by demanding certain properties on the distribution of the values of all sensitive attributes.

Differential Privacy. Differential privacy [8,9] uses a different approach to address problems of anonymity. It is rooted in the observation that all queries in statistical databases necessarily leak information about the individuals over which the statistics where computed, and that this information is dependent on the size and distribution of the data. On the other hand, no query will leak information about a user who is not contained in the database. Hence, the aim of differential privacy is to ensure that each user has essentially the same privacy as if his entry were removed from the database. This is typically achieved by modifying the results of queries against the database by spiking in sufficient amounts of noise. However, this approach does not easily allow to quantify the privacy estimated for a given user in a given database. In addition, the approach cannot protect a user's privacy if an attacker can circumvent the noise injection.

Information Theoretic Measures. Another popular alternative to estimating the size of the anonymity set consists in the use of information theoretic measures, such as the self information, which can be interpreted as the number of yes/no - questions an attacker would have to answer to identify an item in a data set uniquely. Hence, it corresponds to the amount of information, measured in bits, an attacker would need to possess about a user to identify it, or would learn upon identification of the user.

Formally, the self information is defined as the negative logarithm of the probability of a data item: $\mathrm{SI(x)} = -\log(p(x))$. To relate this quantity to the problem of privacy measurement, imagine an attacker who intends to relate the data contained in a data base to a targeted user t. To identify the entry of the database corresponding to u, the attacker models a probability distribution $p(x)$, describing the probability with which he considers a user x contained in the database to be equal to thc targeted user u. Thus a low probability leads to a high anonymity, and corresponds to a large self information. Effectively, this measure quantifies the amount of additional information an attacker would have to obtain to identify a user amongst all candidates from his anonymity set.

To quantify how resistant a given dataset is against such attacks, we can compute the expected value of the self information $H(X) = \sum_{x \in X} p(x) SI(x) = -\sum_{x \in X} p(x) \log(p(x))$ This quantity is known as the entropy of the dataset.

2.1 Proxy Measures for k-Anonymity

In the following, we will describe the privacy measures used in our study. The idea here is to provide a simple and efficiently computable proxy for the size of the anonymity set, similar in spirit to the ideas of k-anonymity and related measures. The simplicity of the measures will greatly simplify discussion of the secure protocols developed later in this manuscript. In addition, we will demonstrate how to implement k-anonymity measurements using our protocol.

z-Scores. Let us first assume that the data is one-dimensional and continuous with mean μ and standard deviation σ. A simple way to approximate anonymity in this scenario consists in answering the question `'how many standard deviations does my value differ from the mean?'` This quantity is known as the **z-score**, with

$$z(x) = \frac{x - \mu}{\sigma}$$

To see that the z-value encodes information about a user's privacy in this scenario, consider Chebyshev's inequality, which states that for the random variable x and $k > 0$

$$P\left(|x - \mu| \geq k\sigma\right) \leq \frac{1}{k^2}$$

Hence, we expect at least $100 \times \left(1 - \frac{1}{k^2}\right)$ percent of the data to fall within k standard deviations from the mean. Roughly speaking, a user with a z-value of 5 can then only expect to hide within 4% of the data, while 96% are concentrated closer to the mean.

In such a context, a user could then consider himself sufficiently anonymous if the magnitude of his z-score falls below a certain threshold t, i.e.

$$|z(x)| = \left|\frac{x - \mu}{\sigma}\right| < t$$

with $t \in \mathbb{R}^+$ chosen by the user. The method can be easily generalized to multi-dimensional data by either combining the deviation from the mean along all dimensions into a single score, or by requiring z-score-bounds for each dimension individually.

Multi-dimensional Histograms. The z-score-based measure is particularly appropriate for distributions concentrated close to the mean with small variance. For highly irregular distributions, such as multi-modal sums of Gaussians, the underlying structure of the distribution might render the user recognizable even if he falls close to the mean. In addition, the measure is not applicable to categorical data. In such cases, we first compute a (multi-dimensional) histogram of the data set. The size of the histogram bucket then carries information about the relative size of the anonymity set.

Histogram-Based Self-information. As described in Sect. 2, the self information $SI(x) = -\log(p(x))$ yields a suitable privacy measure, where large SI values correspond to high degree of anonymity. To apply this measure in practice, we need to specify a model for the probability $p(x)$.

For our scenario, we chose $p = \frac{1}{n \times s_i}$ where n denotes the number of equivalence classes within the database, represented by the number of histogram buckets, and s_i the size of the bucket into which item x falls. It is illustrative to note that the self information then decomposes into a sum of two terms:

$$SI(x) = -\log\left(\frac{1}{n \times s_i}\right) = \log(n \times s_i) = \log(n) + \log(s_i) \quad (1)$$

the first of these terms describes the number of bits required to identify the bucket of the item, the second the number of bits required to identify the item in the bucket.

3 Privately Querying Privacy

The measures described in the previous section can be easily implemented and efficiently computed. But they all require sensitive input from both parties – the end user as well as the database provider. Hence, it might seem as if either one party would have to share private information with the other, or both with a trusted third party.

Our aim in this study is to demonstrate that it is indeed possible to compute privacy measures without any of the parties leaking sensitive information to each other or a third party. This enables users to make informed decisions about sharing their data with service providers without leaking private information before a decision to share has been made. At the same time, it protects the trade secrets of the service provider as well as the privacy of all other users whose data is contained in the database.

3.1 Cryptographic Primitives

Our protocols make use of three main cryptographic primitives: oblivious transfer (OT) [10,23], secure multiparty computation (SMC) [27,28], and private set intersection (PSI) [5,11].

OT methods allow a user, typically called Alice, to request one of multiple pieces of information from another party, usually called Bob, where Bob remains oblivious as to which piece of information was requested. SMC describes a collection of methods that allow multiple parties to jointly compute a function over inputs from the different parties while keeping each parties' input private from all other parties. PSI approaches allow two parties to privately compute the intersection of sets held by the parties.

Our protocols typically assume 'honest, but curious' participants, i.e., each participant is required to provide correct values as input into the protocols, but can be expected to try and infer the input data of the other party. The aim of the protocols is to prevent him from succeeding in this endeavour.

3.2 Private Computation of z-Score-Based Privacy

We first describe how to compute the z-score of a user in a database in a private manner. Here, the user brings his own data into the protocol, while the database provider inputs mean μ and standard deviation σ (generalization to multi-variate quantities is straight-forward). In principle, we could simply implement equation (2.1) using a suitable SMC framework. But while this would guarantee that none of the parties gains knowledge about the input of the other during the computation, it would still be prone to information leakage.

First, and most importantly, the service provider could directly infer the user's supposedly private data from the resulting z-score through knowledge of μ and σ, as

$$x = z(x) \times \sigma + \mu$$

Hence, we need to ensure that the service provider does not learn the result of the z-score computation while performing the SMC. This can easily be achieved in many SMC implementations.

Second, the user could infer the database parameters μ and σ through repeated queries with modified input value:

$$\begin{aligned} z_1 = z(x_1) &= \frac{x_1 - \mu}{\sigma} \\ z_2 = z(x_2) &= \frac{x_2 - \mu}{\sigma} \\ \Rightarrow \sigma &= \frac{x_2 - x_1}{z_2 - z_1} \\ \mu &= x_1 - z_1\sigma \end{aligned}$$

To address this problem, we do not return the z-score from our protocol, but rather only answer whether the z-score is below a threshold t. This does not entirely resolve the problem, as a user could try bisecting queries to determine the input value for which the threshold is crossed. However, it would require a greater number of protocol evaluations. Further steps can be taken to address this scenario, such as a third-party control that limits the number of evaluation requests, or slight random perturbations of the threshold. In addition, the attack becomes much harder to realize for high-dimensional data in a multi-variate setting.

Please note that a similar strategy could be employed by the service provider to compute the input of a user who performs multiple queries against the database. But the protocol can easily be implemented in such a way as to make it challenging for the service provider to decide whether two queries came from the same user, e.g. through the use of a proxy for all network communication.

3.3 Private Computation of Histogram-Based Privacy

In practice, not all values come in the form of continuous quantities that are simply distributed. As described in Sect. 2.1, many such cases can be effectively handled through the use of multi-dimensional histograms. Such techniques can not only handle discrete input quantities, but are also usually more appropriate for continuous distributions that are not essentially concentrated at the mean. In addition, histogram-based methods can further form the basis of information-theoretic privacy metrics, such as the self-information described above.

For discrete features, histograms can be set up in such a way as to preserve the equivalence classes of the original feature by letting each histogram bucket cover exactly one feature value. More commonly, though, each histogram bucket covers multiple values of the original feature. In this case, using a histogram weakens the anonymity guarantees, as we now work with similarity groups instead of true equivalence classes: each histogram bucket now contains points with *similar* values, not necessarily *identical* ones. To give an example, imagine a histogram box for the variable age, covering the range [20–24). If the database contains exactly one entry for each of those ages, a user with age 20 querying his privacy would expect to hide within five users of the same age group, even though only one of those is truly indistinguishable from him. Hence, care has to be taken when setting up the histogram configuration, so that histogram buckets reasonably coincide with anonymity sets.

Multi-dimensional Histogram Approximation. To securely evaluate the size of his similarity group in the database, which might be a multi-dimensional mixture of floating point numbers, integers, quantities on an ordinal scale, and categorical features, we first compute a multi-dimensional histogram for the database. Evaluating the user's privacy in this dataset then becomes a matter of deciding whether the amount of users in the same histogram bucket, i.e., the associated value of that bucket, exceeds a certain threshold t. Deciding this question requires to determine the particular histogram bucket for the user, i.e., the user's index in the histogram, to evaluate the corresponding histogram bucket, and to make a decision based on that value.

Ensuring Privacy of the User. If privacy of the database provider is not an issue, i.e., if an arbitrary amount of information about his database is allowed to leak, privacy of the user can be trivially ensured: the user first receives a copy of the histogram of the database to then evaluate his privacy. In the following, we will refer to the user as *Alice* and to the database provider as *Bob*.

Let Alice's data be denoted by $\boldsymbol{x} := (x_1, \ldots, x_n)$, where $x_i, 1 \leq i \leq n$ is her feature value along dimension i. For each dimension i, Bob has computed a histogram. Let $\#h_i$ denote the number of histogram buckets along dimension i.

If dimension i is categorical in nature (e.g., gender or nationality), the corresponding histogram bucket index is typically computed from a simple feature encoding, where each feature value maps to an integer in the range $[1, \#h_i]$.

If, instead, dimension i has an ordinal scale, the box definitions of the corresponding histogram h_i can be stored as a breakpoint vector

$$h_i := (-\infty, p_{i_1}, \ldots, p_{i_{\#h_i - 1}}, \infty)$$

Alice can then compute her bucket index along dimension i from

$$\mathcal{I}_i = j \Leftrightarrow p_{i_{j-1}} \leq x_i < p_{i_j}$$

Alice then combines all bucket indices along each dimension into a multivariate index $\mathcal{I}_1\mathcal{I}_2 \ldots \mathcal{I}_n$.

Since Alice has received a copy of Bob's histogram in the first step, she can then proceed to evaluate her histogram bucket $b_{\mathcal{I}_1\mathcal{I}_2\ldots\mathcal{I}_n}$, and from the result evaluate the function $b_{\mathcal{I}_1\mathcal{I}_2\ldots\mathcal{I}_n} > t$, where t is her user-defined threshold of acceptance (i.e., the size of her similarity group).

However, this simple protocol has two main issues. First, it requires transmission of the whole histogram, which might be infeasible. Second, it requires Bob to share the distribution of his dataset with Alice.

Improving Privacy of the Database Provider. In practice, Bob will not agree to share the full histogram with Alice. To improve his privacy, we first note that for the computation of Alice's histogram index, it is sufficient to share the feature encodings for all categorical features and the breakpoint vectors for all ordinal ones. From this information, Alice can compute her multivariate histogram index $\mathcal{I}_1\mathcal{I}_2 \ldots \mathcal{I}_n$ just as described above.

To evaluate the privacy decision function $b_{\mathcal{I}_1\mathcal{I}_2\ldots\mathcal{I}_n} > t$ without sharing $\mathcal{I}_1\mathcal{I}_2 \ldots \mathcal{I}_n$ with Bob or $b_{\mathcal{I}_1\mathcal{I}_2\ldots\mathcal{I}_n}$ with Alice, we first transmit t to Bob and let Bob compute the thresholded histogram

$$T_{\mathcal{I}_1\mathcal{I}_2\ldots\mathcal{I}_n} := b_{\mathcal{I}_1\mathcal{I}_2\ldots\mathcal{I}_n} > t \;\forall 1 \leq \mathcal{I}_j \leq \#h_j, j \in [1, n]$$

Alice could then request $T_{\mathcal{I}_1\mathcal{I}_2\ldots\mathcal{I}_n}$ using an efficient 1-out-of-n OT scheme. The result directly tells her whether her privacy requirements are fulfilled[1].

In this scheme, Bob only learns the value t of Alice's privacy threshold, while Alice learns the feature mappings of all categorical features and the histogram breakpoints for all ordinal ones.

In practice, this scheme quickly becomes inefficient, as 1-out-of-n oblivious transfer transmits an amount of data that is linear in n [2]. In our application, n is the total number of histogram buckets. Assuming just 10 dimensions with 100 histogram buckets each, we would need to transmit on the order of $100^{10} = 10^{20}$ bytes, which is clearly infeasible.

Alternatively, Alice and Bob could use a private information retrieval (PIR) protocol [3]. In general, these allow a certain amount of information leakage for Bob while guaranteeing Alice's privacy, but require significantly less data transmission than standard OT protocols [2]. This, however, does not solve the problem for histogram sizes as the one above, where we could not even hope to compute or store the histogram.

Efficient Private Histogram Evaluation. To improve our protocol for large histogram sizes, we note that the boolean function $T_{\mathcal{I}_1\mathcal{I}_2\ldots\mathcal{I}_n} := b_{\mathcal{I}_1\mathcal{I}_2\ldots\mathcal{I}_n} > t$ will generally be very sparse for highly-dimensional data. In fact, in a database with N entries, at most N/t histogram boxes can have a value greater than t. As we assume that each entry in the database represents a person, the total amount of data points can hardly exceed several billion, and will often be much less. Hence, the size of the support of $T_{\mathcal{I}_1\mathcal{I}_2\ldots\mathcal{I}_n}$ is much smaller than the size of the histogram itself.

We can then address the private computation of Alice's value $T_{\mathcal{I}_1\mathcal{I}_2\ldots\mathcal{I}_n}$ through the notion of private set inclusion, a special case of the widely studies private set intersection (PSI)-problem. Here, Alice and Bob have a set of values each and want to privately compute their intersection. In our application, Bob's set consists of all multivariate indices $\mathcal{I}_1\mathcal{I}_2\ldots\mathcal{I}_n$ for which $b_{\mathcal{I}_1\mathcal{I}_2\ldots\mathcal{I}_n} > t$. Alice's set only consists of her own histogram index. If the intersection of both sets is non-empty, we know that for Alice, $b_{\mathcal{I}_1\mathcal{I}_2\ldots\mathcal{I}_n} > t$ holds, and hence her privacy requirements are fulfilled. Otherwise, she concludes that she is insufficiently anonymous.

For such highly asymmetric set sizes, PSI can be reasonably performed in a manner of seconds against databases with millions or even billions of entries, even if Alice uses a mobile device [13]. Such protocols often allow a certain false-positive rate to be more efficient, but these rates can be set to be lower than, say, one in a billion.

Hiding the Distribution of the Database Content. While the scheme described in 3.3 is efficient and private for the user, and hides the occupancy

[1] Please note that the multi-index $\mathcal{I}_1\mathcal{I}_2\ldots\mathcal{I}_n$ has to be converted into a scalar index for standard OT implementations. This can be achieved by, e.g., shifting each $\mathcal{I}_j$ by $\sum_{k=1}^{j-1}\lceil\log_2(\#h_k)\rceil$ bits before combining all into a single number.

of the histogram buckets, it still leaks sensitive data of the database provider. Since the user is provided with the definition of all histogram breakpoints, he can gain significant insight into the data distribution.

In fact, even if Alice can compute $\mathcal{I}_1\mathcal{I}_2\ldots\mathcal{I}_n$ without Bob sharing breakpoint vectors, it still leaks information that Bob wants to keep private. Imagine, for instance, that $\mathcal{I}_1$ evaluates to a very small integer. Alice can then conclude that her value x_1 belongs to the lowest quantiles in Bob's dataset. This would thus inform Alice about the distribution of Bob's data, which he intends to keep private.

To address this problem, we now describe a novel scheme to compute Alice's histogram index $\mathcal{I}_1\mathcal{I}_2\ldots\mathcal{I}_n$, privately for both, Alice and Bob. The resulting scheme is highly efficient and rather simple to implement. Together with the results from Sect. 3.3, this allows an efficient private computation of the privacy test $b_{\mathcal{I}_1\mathcal{I}_2\ldots\mathcal{I}_n} > t$.

To prevent information leakage, Bob first chooses random numbers $\rho_1,\ldots,\rho_n$, with $\rho_i \in [0, \#h_i)$ and computes

$$\hat{T}_{\mathcal{I}_1\mathcal{I}_2\ldots\mathcal{I}_n} := T_{\mathcal{I}_1\oplus_i\rho_1\mathcal{I}_2\oplus_i\rho_2\ldots\mathcal{I}_n\oplus_i\rho_n}$$

where $x \oplus_i y := x + y \mod \#h_i$.

As Alice has no knowledge about the value of the random cyclic index shift ρ_i (which is not reused between requests), evaluation of her box index in the shifted array $\hat{T}$ will not inform her about the corresponding index in the original array, and hence will not leak information about the quantiles.

Secure Multiparty Computation of Histogram Indices. If the histogram breakpoints were public, Alice could iterate the breakpoint vector h_i in sorted order and find the first point for which her value is greater or equal to the breakpoint as describe in Sect. 3.3. Obviously, this would again leak information about the data distribution to Alice.

Instead, Bob now computes for each histogram box b_{ij} along dimension i its left and right boundaries l_{ij}, r_{ij}. He stores these boundaries sorted according to the order of the index-shifted table $\hat{T}$, i.e., ordered according to $1\oplus_i\rho_i,\ldots,\#h_i\oplus_i \rho_i$. To compute her histogram index, Alice needs to compare her value x_i to those endpoints: if $x_i \geq l_{ij}$ and $x_i < r_{ij}$, the histogram index along direction i in the index shifted table is found to be j.

To perform this computation privately, we design an SMC protocol for the comparisons involved.

For the following, fix any dimension i and let k be the number of (finite) breakpoints of h_i. Our protocol can be implemented using any SMC method for the efficient comparison of integer numbers that uses a garbled circuit for the result, such as [15] (see [4] for a recent overview).

We perform all comparisons of Alice's data $\boldsymbol{x}$ to all boundaries of the shifted indices in parallel, but do not disclose the result. Thus, for each dimension i of $\boldsymbol{x}$, we end up with labels $X_0^i,\ldots X_{k+1}^i$ which encode the garbled output of the comparisons $x_i < r_{ij}$ for $0 \leq j \leq k+1$.

Now, the index along dimension i of the interval of the shifted table that contains x can easily be determined as the index j for which $X_j^i = 0$ and $X_{j\oplus_\kappa 1}^i = 1$ (with $\kappa := k+2$). This computation requires one additional gate[2] $\neg X_j^i \wedge X_{j\oplus_\kappa 1}^i$ per interval, where $\oplus_\kappa$ is again interpreted in a cyclic way. Clearly, this can be done for all dimensions in parallel, such that the number of rounds required is small.

Finally, these $n \cdot (k+1)$ values are disclosed to Alice but not to Bob to inform her about her histogram index in the cyclically shifted table. Using the technique described in Sect. 3.3, Alice can finally evaluate the privacy test privately for both her and Bob.

Summary and Security Analysis. We summarize the final protocol and sketch a security analysis, for which we assume the security of the used building blocks: the garbled circuits and the private set intersection. For a schematic description, we refer to Fig. 2.

We assume that the threshold t, the dimension n and (upper bounds on) the number of histogram buckets $\#h_i$ for each dimension is common knowledge. The second information does not need to be made public but it can not be kept entirely secret and hence, we assume that is public knowledge in the analysis.

As the first step, a garbled circuit with inputs $x_1, \ldots, x_n$ of the user and $(r_{i,j\oplus_i\rho_i})_{1\leq i\leq n, 0\leq j\leq \#h_1}$ of the database provider is set up in a way that the database provider does not obtain any information at all, while the user obtains $\mathcal{I}_1 \oplus_1 \rho_1, \ldots, \mathcal{I}_n \oplus_n \rho_n$. As, for all $1 \leq i \leq n$, ρ_i are chosen independently at random from $0, \ldots, \#h_i - 1$, the numbers $\mathcal{I}_i \oplus_1 \rho_i$ are distributed uniformly at random in $0, \ldots, \#h_i - 1$. Furthermore, the database provider will chose different random numbers if the user makes several queries. Hence there is no (additional) information that the user learns through running several rounds of the protocol. Please note that, if $\#h_i$ would not be made public, the user could infer information on the $\#h_i$ from his distribution of the $\mathcal{I}_i \oplus_i \rho_i$ values. Hence, it cannot be kept entirely private.

Finally, a private set intersection with inputs $\{(\mathcal{I}_1 \oplus_1 \rho_1, \ldots, \mathcal{I}_n \oplus_n \rho_n)\}$ of the user and $\{(j_1, \ldots, j_n) \mid b_{j_1\oplus_1\rho_1,\ldots,j_n\oplus_n\rho_n} > t\}$ of the database provider so that the database provider does not obtain any information, while the user only receives the information whether $\{(\mathcal{I}_1 \oplus_1 \rho_1, \ldots, \mathcal{I}_n \oplus_n \rho_n)\}$ belongs to $\{(j_1, \ldots, j_n \mid b_{j_1\oplus_1\rho_1,\ldots,j_n\oplus_n\rho_n} > t\}$, i.e. exactly the information which we assumed that the database provider is willing to share with the user.

Clearly, by repeating the protocol several times, the user can obtain some information on the distribution in the database. To be precise, he can try to determine which cells of the histogram would fulfill his anonymity threshold by brute force. For realistically sized histograms, however, gaining information

[2] Notice that it might, at first glance, seem reasonable to use a simpler and more efficient XOR instead of $\neg X_j^i \wedge X_{j\oplus_\kappa 1}^i$; unfortunately, this does not work because it results in a value of 1 at the boundary of the last to the first interval and hence would reveal ρ_i.

about a non-trivial percentage of the histogram would require an infeasible number of rounds, and the number of repetitions can be monitored by the database provider to prevent brute forcing.

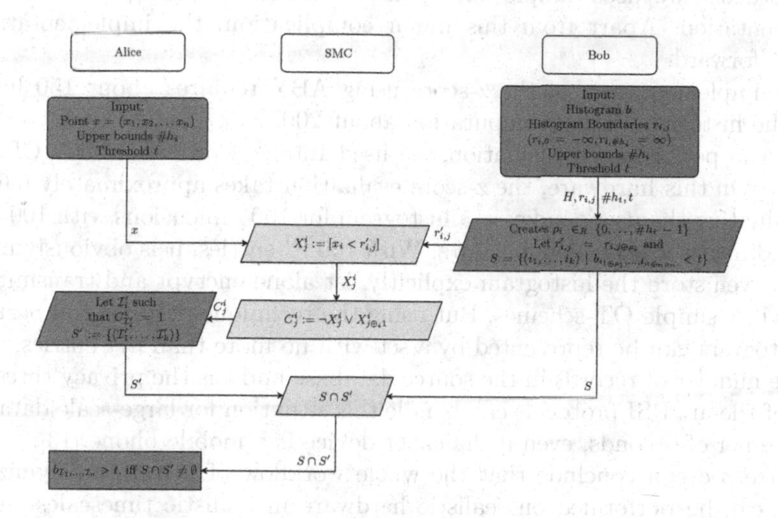

Fig. 2. Schematic description of the protocol. To clarify the communication, we used additional symbols $r'_{i,j} := r_{i,j\oplus_i\rho_i}$, $C^i_j := \neg X^i_j \vee X^i_{j\oplus_i 1}$, $\mathcal{I}'$ for Alice' shifted index and S' the set containing exactly Alice' shifted index.

3.4 Private Computation of Self-information-Based Privacy

The protocol can easily be adapted to base the privacy estimation on other metrics that can be independently evaluated for each histogram bucket. For instance, with the simple probability model described above (derived from the number of groups and the number of elements in the given group), we can compute the self-information from Eq. (1):

$$SI(x) = -\log\left(\frac{1}{n \times s_i}\right) = \log(n \times s_i) = \log(n) + \log(s_i)$$

where n is the number of histogram buckets and s_i the number of elements in bucket i. Since all members of a histogram bucket share the same SI-value according to this model, the service provider can just as easily fill table $T_{\mathcal{I}_1\mathcal{I}_2\ldots\mathcal{I}_n}$ with the SI-values, allowing the user to threshold based on self-information instead of the size of the anonymity set (as both are easily related in this model).

4 Performance Evaluation

To evaluate the performance of our method on realistic data sizes, we developed a prototypical implementation of our protocols based on the open source ABY-library [6]. Our evaluation is not meant to provide an in-depth view on the scaling behavior, but rather merely serves to demonstrate that the running times achievable are compatible with real-world applications.

To simplify efficient representation of the real-valued quantities required by our protocols, we used simple fixed-point arithmetic on integer values in our implementation. Apart from this minor complication, the implementation is straight-forward.

Our implementation of the z-score using ABY requires about 150 lines of code, the histogram index computation about 200.

For the performance evaluation, we used Intel® Core™ i7-8650 CPUs at 1.9 GHz. On this hardware, the z-score evaluation takes approximately 0.6 s.

Evaluating the user's index in a histogram for 100 dimensions with 100 buckets per dimension takes roughly 1.6 s. With 100^{100} entries, it is obviously impossible to even store the histogram explicitly, let alone encrypt and transmit it as required by simple OT-schemes. But using the technique described in Sect. 3.3, the histogram can be represented by a set with no more than n/t entries, where n is the number of records in the source database and t is the privacy threshold. State-of-the-art PSI protocols can handle this situation for large-scale databases in a manner of seconds, even if the client device is a mobile phone [13].

Hence, we can conclude that the whole workflow of private anonymization queries can be performed on realistic hardware in realistic timescales (several seconds) even for realistic database sizes of several million to billions of entries for highly dimensional datasets with finely resolved histograms.

5 Conclusions

A side-effect of recent breakthroughs in data storage and transfer, big data analysis, and machine learning is a growing concern for privacy in an increasingly data-driven world. As many modern services, ranging from convenient to irreplaceable, rely on the availability of user-provided data, simply cutting off or anonymizing all data transfer cannot be the solution. Instead, we believe that providing a user with sufficient information to make an informed choice of whether to share his data or not will be one key aspect of future privacy-aware solutions. This necessitates the usage of suitable privacy metrics, which are an active field of research in the literature. In this work we have shown how a fundamental hen-and-egg problem underlying the evaluation of privacy norms in practice can be approached, namely the question of how to evaluate a user's privacy without leaking either his information, nor that of the service provider, before a conscious decision to share data has been made. The techniques described in this work have been developed based on simple privacy estimates, but are abstract enough to generalize to wider classes of privacy metrics. They are amenable to efficient implementations using standard SMC and PSI toolkits which do not require deep insight into the cryptographic details, and can be performed in realistic running times on realistic hardware.

Funding. This work was supported by the German Ministry of Education and Research through the DaSoMan-project [16KIS0804 to AKH].

References

1. Aggarwal, C.C.: On k-anonymity and the curse of dimensionality. In: Proceedings of the 31st International Conference on Very Large Data Bases, VLDB 2005, pp. 901–909. VLDB Endowment (2005). http://dl.acm.org/citation.cfm?id=1083592.1083696
2. Aguilar Melchor, C., Barrier, J., Fousse, L., Killijian, M.O.: XPIR: private information retrieval for everyone. Proc. Privacy Enhan. Technol. **2016**, 155–174 (2016)
3. Chor, B., Kushilevitz, E., Goldreich, O., Sudan, M.: Private information retrieval. J. ACM **45**(6), 965–981 (1998). https://doi.org/10.1145/293347.293350
4. Couteau, G.: New protocols for secure equality test and comparison. In: Proceedings of the Applied Cryptography and Network Security - 16th International Conference, ACNS 2018, Leuven, Belgium, July 2–4, 2018, pp. 303–320 (2018). https://doi.org/10.1007/978-3-319-93387-0_16
5. Dachman-Soled, D., Malkin, T., Raykova, M., Yung, M.: Efficient robust private set intersection. In: Abdalla, M., Pointcheval, D., Fouque, P.-A., Vergnaud, D. (eds.) ACNS 2009. LNCS, vol. 5536, pp. 125–142. Springer, Heidelberg (2009). https://doi.org/10.1007/978-3-642-01957-9_8
6. Demmler, D., Schneider, T., Zohner, M.: ABY - a framework for efficient mixed-protocol secure two-party computation. In: 22nd Annual Network and Distributed System Security Symposium (NDSS 2015). Internet Society, February 2015. http://tubiblio.ulb.tu-darmstadt.de/101761/
7. Diggelmann, O., Cleis, M.N.: How the right to privacy became a human right. Hum. Rights Law Rev. **14**(3), 441–458 (2014)
8. Alvim, M.S., Chatzikokolakis, K., McIver, A., Morgan, C., Palamidessi, C., Smith, G.: Differential privacy (2020). https://doi.org/10.1007/978-3-319-96131-6_23
9. Dwork, C.: Differential privacy: a survey of results. In: Agrawal, M., Du, D., Duan, Z., Li, A. (eds.) TAMC 2008. LNCS, vol. 4978, pp. 1–19. Springer, Heidelberg (2008). https://doi.org/10.1007/978-3-540-79228-4_1
10. Even, S., Goldreich, O., Lempel, A.: A randomized protocol for signing contracts. Commun. ACM **28**(6), 637–647 (1985)
11. Freedman, M.J., Nissim, K., Pinkas, B.: Efficient private matching and set intersection. In: Cachin, C., Camenisch, J.L. (eds.) EUROCRYPT 2004. LNCS, vol. 3027, pp. 1–19. Springer, Heidelberg (2004). https://doi.org/10.1007/978-3-540-24676-3_1
12. Gymrek, M., McGuire, A.L., Golan, D., Halperin, E., Erlich, Y.: Identifying personal genomes by surname inference. Science **339**(6117), 321–324 (2013)
13. Kiss, Á., Liu, J., Schneider, T., Asokan, N., Pinkas, B.: Private set intersection for unequal set sizes with mobile applications. In: Proceedings on Privacy Enhancing Technologies, vol. 4, pp. 177–197 (2017). https://doi.org/10.1515/popets-2017-0044
14. Kolesnikov, V., Kumaresan, R., Rosulek, M., Trieu, N.: Efficient batched oblivious PRF with applications to private set intersection. In: Proceedings of the 2016 ACM SIGSAC Conference on Computer and Communications Security, CCS 2016, pp. 818–829. ACM, New York (2016). https://doi.org/10.1145/2976749.2978381, http://doi.acm.org/10.1145/2976749.2978381
15. Kolesnikov, V., Sadeghi, A., Schneider, T.: Improved garbled circuit building blocks and applications to auctions and computing minima. In: Proceedings of the Cryptology and Network Security, 8th International Conference, CANS 2009, Kanazawa, Japan, 12–14 December 2009. pp. 1–20 (2009). https://doi.org/10.1007/978-3-642-10433-6_1

16. Kotsogiannis, I., Tao, Y., He, X., Fanaeepour, M., Machanavajjhala, A., Hay, M., Miklau, G.: Privatesql: a differentially private SGL query engine. Proc. VLDB Endow. **12**(11), 1371–1384 (2019)
17. Li, N., Li, T., Venkatasubramanian, S.: t-Closeness: privacy beyond k-anonymity and l-diversity. In: 2007 IEEE 23rd International Conference on Data Engineering, pp. 106–115, April 2007. https://doi.org/10.1109/ICDE.2007.367856
18. Li, S., Wang, D., Dai, Y.: Efficient secure multiparty computational geometry. Chin. J. Electr. **19**(2), 324–328 (2010)
19. Liu, X., Li, S., Liu, J., Chen, X., Xu, G.: Secure multiparty computation of a comparison problem. SpringerPlus 5 (2016). https://doi.org/10.1186/s40064-016-3061-0, https://pdfs.semanticscholar.org/454f/f4c920ea2dd4ea74cc4ac3e7114ff016c582.pdf
20. Machanavajjhala, A., Kifer, D., Gehrke, J., Venkitasubramaniam, M.: L-diversity: privacy beyond k-anonymity. ACM Trans. Knowl. Discov. Data **1**(1), March 2007. https://doi.org/10.1145/1217299.1217302, http://doi.acm.org/10.1145/1217299.1217302
21. Naor, M., Pinkas, B.: Oblivious transfer and polynomial evaluation. In: Proceedings of the Thirty-first Annual ACM Symposium on Theory of Computing. STOC 1999, pp. 245–254. ACM, New York (1999). https://doi.org/10.1145/301250.301312, http://doi.acm.org/10.1145/301250.301312
22. Narayanan, A., Shmatikov, V.: Robust de-anonymization of large sparse datasets. In: 2008 IEEE Symposium on Security and Privacy (SP 2008), pp. 111–125, May 2008. https://doi.org/10.1109/SP.2008.33
23. Rabin, M.O.: How to exchange secrets with oblivious transfer. Technical Report TR-81
24. Sweeney, L.: K-anonymity: a model for protecting privacy. Int. J. Uncertain. Fuzziness Knowl.-Based Syst. **10**(5), 557–570 (2002). https://doi.org/10.1142/S0218488502001648, http://dx.doi.org/10.1142/S0218488502001648
25. Wagner, I.: Genomic privacy metrics: a systematic comparison. In: 2015 IEEE Security and Privacy Workshops, pp. 50–59, May 2015. https://doi.org/10.1109/SPW.2015.15
26. Wagner, I., Eckhoff, D.: Technical privacy metrics: a systematic survey. ACM Comput. Surv. 51(3), 57:1–57:38 (2018). https://doi.org/10.1145/3168389, http://doi.acm.org/10.1145/3168389
27. Yao, A.C.: Protocols for secure computations. In: 23rd Annual Symposium on Foundations of Computer Science (SFCS 1982), pp. 160–164, November 1982. https://doi.org/10.1109/SFCS.1982.38
28. Yao, A.C.: How to generate and exchange secrets. In: 27th Annual Symposium on Foundations of Computer Science (SFCS 1986), pp. 162–167, October 1986. https://doi.org/10.1109/SFCS.1986.25

Brief Announcement: On the Distributed Construction of Stable Networks in Polylogarithmic Parallel Time

Matthew Connor(✉)

Department of Computer Science, University of Liverpool, Liverpool, UK
M.Connor3@liverpool.ac.uk

Abstract. We study the class of networks which can be created in polylogarithmic parallel time by *network constructors* [O. Michail, P. Spirakis, Distributed Computing 29(3), 207–237 (2016)]. We prove that the class of trees where each node has any $k \geq 2$ children can be constructed in $O(\log n)$ parallel time with high probability. We show that constructing networks which are k-regular is $\Omega(n)$ time, but a minimal relaxation to (l, k)-regular networks, where $l = k - 1$ can be constructed in polylogarithmic parallel time for any fixed k, where $k > 2$. We further demonstrate that when the finite-state assumption is relaxed and k is allowed to grow with n, then $k = \log \log n$ acts as a threshold above which network construction is again polynomial time. We use this to provide a partial characterisation of the class of polylogarithmic time network constructors.

Keywords: Population protocol · Distributed network construction · Polylogarithmic time protocol · Spanning tree · Regular network

1 Introduction

Passively dynamic networks are an important type of dynamic network in which the network dynamics are *external* to the algorithm and are a property of the environment in which a given system operates. Wireless sensor networks in which individual sensors are carried by autonomous entities, such as animals, or are deployed in a dynamic environment, such as the flow of a river, are examples of passively dynamic networks. In terms of modelling such systems, the network dynamics are usually assumed to be controlled by an *adversary scheduler* who has exclusive control over the interaction or communication sequence among the computational entities. Population protocols are a prominent example of a model for passively dynamic networks [1].

Recent progress has highlighted the interesting trade-offs between local space of the entities and the running time of protocols. Berenbrink, Giakkoupis and

This reports on joint work with O. Michail and P. Spirakis which has appeared in [3].

© Springer Nature Switzerland AG 2021
G. D'Angelo and O. Michail (Eds.): ALGOCLOUD 2021, LNCS 13084, pp. 73–80, 2021.
https://doi.org/10.1007/978-3-030-93043-1_5

Kling [2] designed a space optimal ($O(\log \log n)$ states) leader election protocol, which stabilises in $O(\log n)$ parallel time.

The other main type of dynamic networks, with respect to who controls the changes in the network topology, are *actively dynamic networks*. In such networks, the algorithm is able to either implicitly change the sequence of interactions by controlling the mobility of the entities or explicitly modify the network structure by creating and destroying communication links at will. Very recently, Michail et al. introduced a fully distributed model for computation and reconfiguration in actively dynamic networks [4].

An interesting alternative family of dynamic networks rises when one considers a mixture of the passive network dynamics of the environment and the active dynamics resulting from an algorithm that can partially control the network changes or that can fix network structures that the environment is unable to affect. This is naturally motivated by molecular interactions where, for example, proteins can bind to each other, forming structures and maintaining their stability despite the dynamicity of the solution in which they reside. Michail and Spirakis [5] introduced and studied such an abstract model of distributed network construction, called the *network constructors* model, where the network dynamicity is the same as in population protocols but now the finite-state entities can additionally activate and deactivate pairwise connections upon their interactions. It was shown that very complex global networks can be formed stably, despite the dynamicity of the environment.

1.1 Our Contribution

We investigate which families of networks can be stably constructed by a distributed computing system in polylogarithmic parallel time.

Our protocols assume the existence of a leader node. A node x is a *leader node* if in the initial configuration, all $u \in V \setminus \{x\}$, where V is the set of all nodes, are in state q_0 and x is in state $s \neq q_0$.

We first study the *k-children spanning tree* problem, where the goal is to construct a tree where each node has, at most $k \geq 2$, children. We show that it is possible to solve this problem for any k in $O(\log n)$ time with high probability. We then show that network constructors which create k-regular graphs necessarily take $\Omega(n)$ time. However, with minimal relaxation to $(k-1, k)$-regular networks, the problem can be solved for any constant $k \geq 2$ in polylogarithmic time. We examine this as a special case of the (l, k)-*Regular Network* problem, where the goal is to construct a spanning network in which every node has at least $l < k$ and at most k connections, where $2 < k < n$. We then transition to experimental analysis of the protocol, which not only provides evidence of the sharp contrast of the minimal relaxation but also reveals a threshold value for k, beyond which the problem reverts to polynomial time. We use this knowledge to propose a first partial characterisation of the set of polylogarithmic time network constructors. We leave providing formal bounds as an open problem.

In Sect. 2, we formally define the model of network constructors and the network construction problems that are considered in this work. In Sect. 3, we study the k-children spanning tree problem and provide the lower bound for k-regular networks. We then present a protocol for the (l, k)-regular network problem and our experimental analysis, culminating in partial characterisation.

2 Materials and Methods

Definition 1. *A* Network Constructor *(NET) is a distributed protocol defined by a 4-tuple* $(Q, q_0, Q_{out}, \delta)$*, where* Q *is a finite set of* node-states, $q_0 \in Q$ *is the* initial node-state, $Q_{out} \subseteq Q$ *is the set of* output node-states, *and* $\delta : Q \times Q \times \{0,1\} \rightarrow Q \times Q \times \{0,1\}$ *is the* transition function.

A *configuration* is a mapping $C : V_I \cup E_I \rightarrow Q \cup \{0,1\}$ specifying the state of each node and each edge of the interaction graph. The output of an execution $C_0, C_1, \ldots$ is said to *stabilize* (or *converge*) to a graph G if there exists some step $t \geq 0$ such that (abbreviated "s.t." in several places) $G(C_i) = G$ for all $i \geq t$, i.e., from step t and onwards, the output graph remains unchanged. Every such configuration C_i, for $i \geq t$ is called *output stable.* The *running time* (or *time to convergence*) of an execution is defined as the minimum such t (or ∞ if no such t exists). Throughout the paper, whenever we study the running time of a NET, we assume that interactions are chosen by a *uniform random scheduler*, which, in every step, selects independently and uniformly at random one of the $|E_I| = n(n-1)/2$ possible interactions. In this case, the running time becomes a random variable (abbreviated "r.v." throughout) X and our goal is to obtain bounds on the expectation $E[X]$ of X. Note that the uniform random scheduler is fair with probability 1.

In this work, "time" is treated as sequential in our analyses, i.e., a time step consists of a single interaction selected by the scheduler. Such a sequential estimate can be easily translated to some estimate of parallel time. For example, assuming that $\Theta(n)$ interactions occur in parallel in every step, one could obtain an estimation of parallel time by dividing sequential time by n. All results are given in parallel time.

Definition 2. *We say that an execution of a NET on* n *nodes* constructs a graph *(or* network*)* G*, if its output stabilises to a graph isomorphic to* G.

Definition 3. *We say that a protocol* P constructs a graph language L*, if in every execution* P *constructs a graph* $G \in L$ *and for all* G*, there exists an execution of* P*, which constructs* G.

We now provide formal definitions for all of the classes of networks considered in this paper.

k-Children Spanning Tree: The goal is to construct a spanning tree where each individual element has at most $k \in \mathbb{N}$ children.

(l, k)-Regular Network: A spanning network where for any $l, k \in \mathbb{N}$ where $l < k$, nodes with degree $d < l$ form a clique and all others have a degree of at least l and at most k.

3 Results

3.1 Polylogarithmic Time Protocols for k-Children Spanning Trees

In this section, we study the complexity of the k-Children Spanning Tree problem. We give a protocol (Algorithm 1) and show that it has a running time of $O(\log n)$ parallel time with high probability.

Algorithm 1. *k-Slot protocol*

$Q = \{F, L_0, L_1, \ldots, L_k, O_0, O_1, \ldots, O_k\}$
δ:

$(L_x, F, 0) \rightarrow (L_{x+1}, O_0, 1)$ for $x < k$
$(O_y, F, 0) \rightarrow (O_{y+1}, O_0, 1)$ for $y < k$

In the above protocol, the F state corresponds to being a node, which is not a member of the tree. L_i corresponds to the *leader* node, which acts as the root of the tree, and O_i to non-leader nodes in the tree, where i represents the number of children of a given node. We assume that for every execution of Algorithm 1 on a population P of n nodes, $n-1$ nodes are initialised to the state F and one node is initialised to the state L_0.

We begin by proving that Algorithm 1 stably constructs the graph language $T_k = \{G | G \text{ is a rooted tree and } \forall u \in P \implies \Delta^+(u) \leq k\}$, where $\Delta^+(u)$ is defined as the number of children of the node u and $k \geq 2$. We then show that this is accomplished in $O(\log n)$ parallel time. Then, we show that this bound holds with high probability.

Lemma 1. *Under Algorithm 1, the connected component S, defined as the leader node and all nodes connected to the leader either directly or indirectly through some other nodes, is eventually spanning.*

Lemma 2. *For all executions of Algorithm 1 on the population P of n nodes, it stabilises to some $G \in T_k$ where $|V(G)| = n$.*

Lemma 3. *For all $G \in T_k$, there is an execution of Algorithm 1, which stabilises on G when starting on a population P of size $n = |V(G)|$.*

Theorem 1. *Algorithm 1 stably constructs the graph language T_k.*

We now show that Algorithm 1 constructs T_k in $O(\log n)$ time w.h.p by considering executions where $k = 2$. Executions where $k > 2$ are necessarily faster, as they have more open slots per node.

Lemma 4. *Let $G \in T_2$ of n nodes. The number of available nodes $\alpha(G) = \lfloor |G|/2 \rfloor + 1$.*

Let the probablistic process P be an execution of Algorithm 1 for $k = 2$ with the following scheduling restriction: If at any point during the execution of Algorithm 1 two nodes x and y have exactly one child, disconnect that child of x or y, which is a leaf, and connect it to the other node. If both are leaves, pick one at random.

Lemma 5. *The expected time to convergence of the probabalistic process P is $O(\log n)$.*

Lemma 6. *The running time of P is the worst case running time for Algorithm 1.*

Lemma 7. *For each time step in Algorithm 1, the probability of any node in the set of unconnected nodes U connecting to the tree is at least $2\frac{|U|}{n}$.*

Lemma 8. *For Algorithm 1, the number of time steps until convergence is $O(\log n)$ w.h.p.*

Theorem 2. *Algorithm 1 stably constructs the graph language T_k in $O(\log n)$ time w.h.p.*

3.2 Time Thresholds for (l, k)-Regular Networks

In this section, we present our solution for the (l, k)-Regular Network problem for $l = k - 1$, the *Cross-edges Tree* protocol. We first show that a *k-regular network*, defined as a network where each node has a degree exactly equal to k, cannot be constructed in polylogarithmic time. We then show via experimental analysis that this impossibility result does not hold for the minimal relaxation of (l, k)-Regular Networks when k is a constant and $l = k - 1$. Finally, we demonstrate that when k exceeds the threshold of $\log\log n$, the protocol itself is no longer in the polylogarithmic time class. Note that from now on, k refers to the *degree* of a node, not the *number of children*.

Theorem 3. *Any protocol which constructs a k-regular network where $k < n$ has a running time of $\Omega(n)$.*

In light of the above impossibility, we now give our protocol (Algorithm 2) for the (l, k)-Regular Network problem when $l = k - 1$. Note that only connecting to F nodes can raise a degree to k; this is to guarantee that there is no scenario where a partial network which unconnected nodes cannot connect to forms.

Algorithm 2. *Cross-edges Tree*

$Q = \{F, L_0, L_1, \ldots, L_k, O_0, O_1, \ldots, O_k\}$
δ:

$(L_x, F, 0) \rightarrow (L_{x+1}, O_0, 1)$ for $x < k$
$(O_y, F, 0) \rightarrow (O_{y+1}, O_0, 1)$ for $y < k$
$(L_x, O_y, 0) \rightarrow (L_{x+1}, O_{y+1}, 1)$ for $x, y < (k-1)$
$(O_y, O_z, 0) \rightarrow (O_{y+1}, O_{z+1}, 1)$ for $y, z < (k-1)$

The Cross-edges Tree protocol adds additional rules, allowing leaves within a tree to connect to other nodes within the tree as though they are candidates for becoming children.

Stabilisation Conditions of the (l, k)-Regular Network. To implement a simulator that can provide results efficiently, we had to define and prove conditions which, when fulfilled, ensure that the protocol is stable. The following theorem states the condition under which the protocol is stable.

Theorem 4. *For $n > k > 3$, at most, $n - k - 2$ nodes have a degree of either k or $k - 1$ and $l \leq k - 2$ nodes are of a degree of at least 1 and at most $k - 2$.*

We now provide the results of simulating the protocol for $k = 3$. We used the same conditions as in the other running time experiments, executing the protocol 10 times for each population size n, where $n = 10 + 6t$, where t is the test number from 0 to 199. The results are given in Fig. 1.

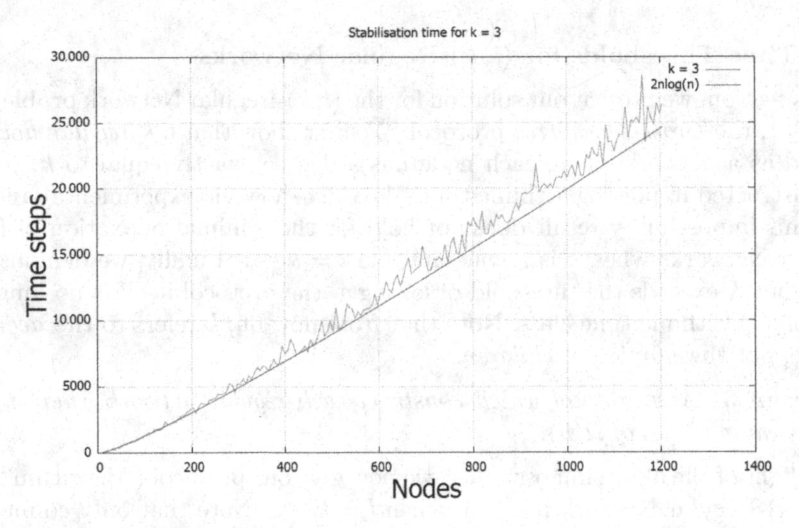

Fig. 1. Running time of the protocol for $k = 3$, compared with a polylogarithmic function.

The running time is difficult to prove formally. This is because random variables are used, which represent the number of nodes with a given degree in a given time step. Their values depend on the values of all random variables in the previous time step. We, therefore, turn our focus to experiments based on measuring the impact of the value of k on the running time of the protocol.

We measured the running time of our Cross-edges Tree protocol for different network sizes. The results below (Fig. 2) show that a higher value of k has little effect on the running time until k exceeds $\log \log n$.

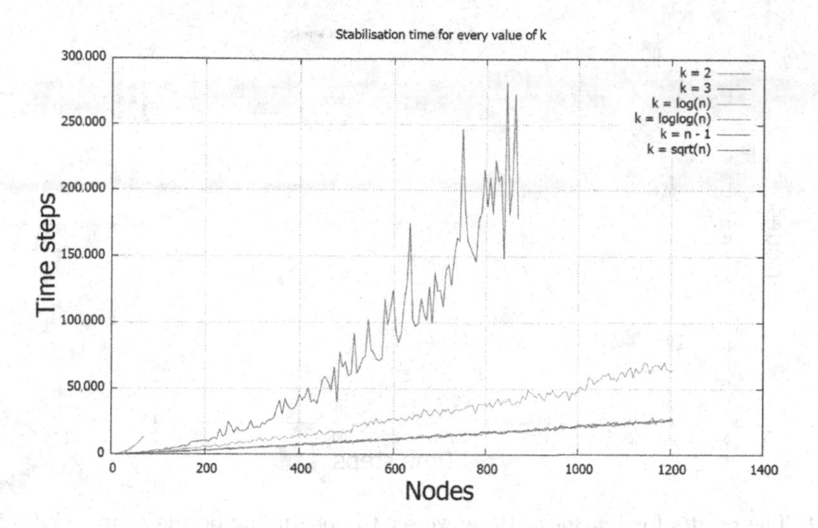

Fig. 2. The effect of k on the running time of the protocol.

To investigate why the protocol slows down dramatically after this point, we ran experiments where we stored the number of nodes with specific degrees in each time step. We executed the protocol with 200 nodes, and ran 10 iterations. These degrees were set to 0, 1, $k/2$, $k-1$, and k.

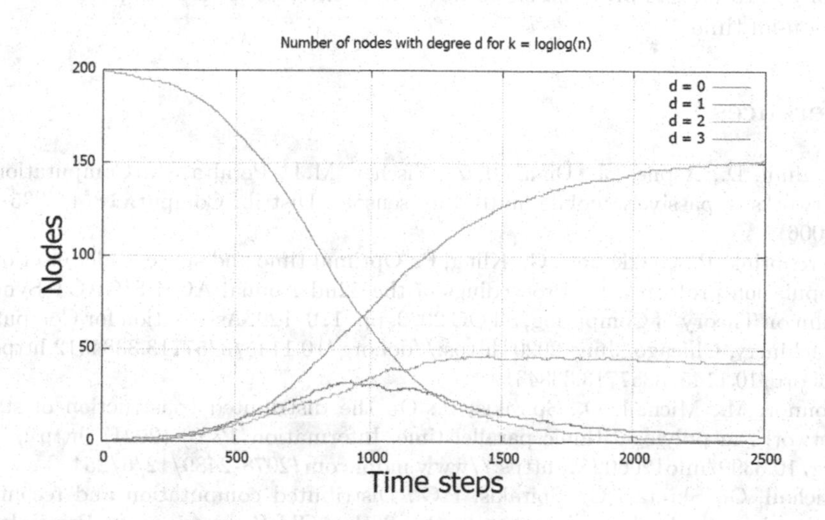

Fig. 3. The results for $k = \log\log n$. Note the difference in the axes labels.

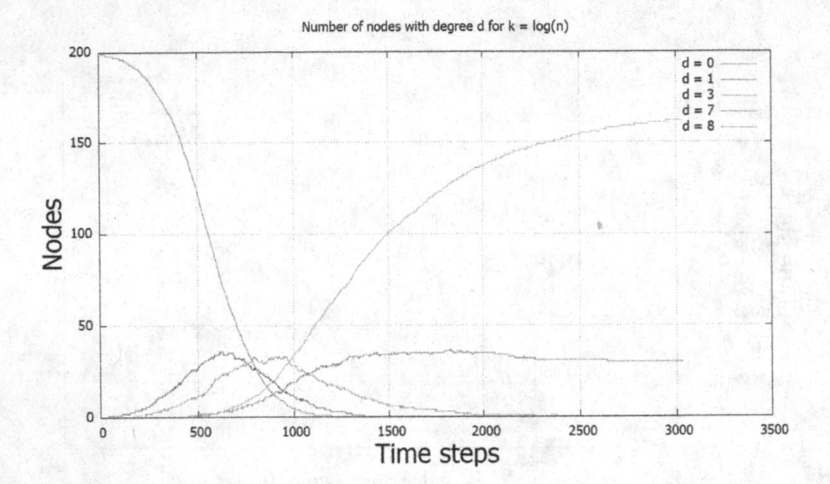

Fig. 4. The results for $k = \log n$. Here, we see the beginning of a leftwards shift of the lines, and an upwards shift in $d = k$.

We collected results for $k = \log\log n$ (Fig. 3), and $k = \log n$ (Fig. 4). The results show that the cause seems to be a large reduction in the number of nodes, which are in the $k - 1$ state as k grows as a fraction of n. They suggest that when the fraction of $k - 1$ nodes is below some fraction between 1/4 and 1/8 of the total, the protocol slows down and enters the class of protocols with polynomial time.

References

1. Angluin, D., Aspnes, J., Diamadi, Z., Fischer, M.J., Peralta, R.: Computation in networks of passively mobile finite-state sensors. Distrib. Comput. **18**(4), 235–253 (2006)
2. Berenbrink, P., Giakkoupis, G., Kling, P.: Optimal time and space leader election in population protocols. In: Proceedings of the 52nd Annual ACM SIGACT Symposium on Theory of Computing, STOC 2020, pp. 119–129. Association for Computing Machinery, Chicago, June 2020. https://doi.org/10.1145/3357713.3384312,https://doi.org/10.1145/3357713.3384312
3. Connor, M., Michail, O., Spirakis, P.: On the distributed construction of stable networks in polylogarithmic parallel time. Information **12**(6) (2021). https://doi.org/10.3390/info12060254, https://www.mdpi.com/2078-2489/12/6/254
4. Michail, O., Skretas, G., Spirakis, P.G.: Distributed computation and reconfiguration in actively dynamic networks. In: 39th ACM Symposium on Principles of Distributed Computing (PODC). ACM (2020)
5. Michail, O., Spirakis, P.G.: Simple and efficient local codes for distributed stable network construction. Distrib. Comput.**29**(3), 207–237 (2016)

Author Index

Acikalin, Utku Umur 38
Althaus, Ernst 56

Caskurlu, Bugra 38
Connor, Matthew 73

Hildebrandt, Andreas 56
Hildebrandt, Anna Katharina 56

Kamali, Shahin 1

Lys, Léonard 18

Micoulet, Arthur 18

Nikbakht, Pooya 1

Potop-Butucaru, Maria 18

Subramani, K. 38

Wojciechowski, Piotr 38

Printed in the United States
by Baker & Taylor Publisher Services

Printed in the United States
by Baker & Taylor Publisher Services